Only a Thought Away

A personal story of bereavement and communication beyond death

Angela Howard

Quacks Books
Q

© Angela Howard 2010

ISBN 978-1-904446-28-6

British Library Cataloguing in Publication Data
Angela Howard 2010
Only a Thought Away

Printed and published by
Quacks Books
Petergate
York YO1 7HU

This book is dedicated –

to Martin, and all those in the world beyond death who are linked with us on Earth by love and a desire to help and inspire us, and to Paul Lambillion and all those who are using their God-given mediumistic gifts to facilitate communication.

I look forward to the day when communication between the worlds is considered natural and normal.

I should like to thank Paul Lambillion for allowing Martin to communicate with me through him. And I should like to thank Martin for his continuing love and inspiration.

I am immensely grateful to my friend Rosalind Smith for editing the book. This has involved many hours of painstaking work during which she has remained good humoured and positive. My thanks to all who have contributed, and to the friends who read the typescript as it grew, and gave valuable criticism; also to Tim Pinney who took all the photographs which are dated 2009. Special thanks to Beryl Spence for helping with the editing process, and to Sylvia Izzard, both of whom listened to my grumbles and encouraged me to keep going.

Contents

Foreword	v
Introduction	vii

Part I

1.	Endings and beginnings	3
2.	About us	7
3.	A journey with cancer	21
4.	A Green burial	35
5.	In the bleak mid-winter	42
6.	"I'm only a thought away"	53
7.	"They showed me a map"	72
8.	"OK, step through"	82
9.	New life at the pottery	99
10.	Sylvia and Jim: Eileen and Ernie	108
11.	Experiencing bereavement	128

Part II

12.	Mediumship, communication and the problems	145
13.	"Nothing in life comes up to the immense joy of dying"	180
14.	"Spiritual beings on a human journey"	218

Booklist	241
Quaker Terminology	246

Foreword

This is a remarkable book, inspired by the communications that Angela has received from her husband Martin since his death in 2003. Towards the end of his life, Martin developed a deep fascination for the art of pottery, becoming an accomplished potter himself. Memorably in these communications he describes how we are all complex and composite beings and how the personality is just the glaze on the pot.

In writing this book Angela herself has given us two pots. The first of these takes as its clay the story of her life with Martin, his death and the continuing connection between them afterwards. It is deeply felt and full of illumination. Angela has had the courage to venture into areas which she might have preferred to keep private, but which needed to be disclosed for the pot to take true shape. She also provides valuable advice on experiencing bereavement and responding to those in mourning.

The second pot comes from the clay of other people's experiences and writings. Angela provides us with an excellent overview of psychic phenomena since the mid-19th century, thereby, as it were, revealing the mould into which the first pot was cast. She also reminds us of the deeply mystical nature of early Quaker experience, and that what we regard as extraordinary and paranormal was once the ordinary and the normal, although invested with great significance, as part of the seamless fabric of human existence.

In our rational scientific age it is understandable that we should be sceptical of things we cannot understand, but we are the losers if we deny them altogether, hush them up or casually assert that we will one day have an explanation. An experience such as Angela has had with the communications from Martin channelled through Paul Lambillion provides us with a wealth of evidence, and also of wisdom and inspiration. That these word for word transcripts can be matter-of-fact and full of the ordinary little exchanges one finds between a couple, somehow makes them all the more convincing and endearing. Everywhere are little touches that have the unmistakable ring of authenticity, like a perfectly thrown and fired pot.

To dismiss these communications as some kind of extended telepathy raises a whole new set of questions, for it shows how deeply we must be communicating with one another all the time at an unseen level in a way for which modern science has no explanation. But more than that, it is the *quality* of the communications that is so convincing, and here I can only invite the reader to plunge in.

This book marks another important chapter in the brief and impressive life of the Quaker Fellowship for Afterlife Studies, founded by Angela and Martin and four like-minded Friends in 2000, and for which Angela has done so much to carry forward as clerk. May it and this book indeed act as the kind of "communicating door" Angela has so much wanted between the world of psychic experiences and contemporary Quakerism in Britain, where interest in such experiences tends to be so muted. *Only a Thought Away* has a great deal to offer to the interested newcomer to this field; to those who have had powerful, out of the ordinary experiences and who wish to place them in some wider and meaningful context; and to those already familiar with the psychic world, who will find all sorts of fresh gems studding the mysterious pot that means so much to them.

Jan Arriens, February 2010

Introduction

*We are not so much human beings on a
spiritual journey as spiritual beings on a
human journey.*

Teilhard de Chardin

My husband, Martin, was diagnosed with cancer in 2002. For fourteen months he worked to regain his health through the use of alternative therapies but died feeling he'd failed. The early chapters of the book tell the story of Martin's illness and death and the wonderful support we had at this time from family and friends.

A month after he died, I visited Paul Lambillion, a healer and spiritual counsellor who had given Martin healing. Through his mediumistic ability Paul became aware of Martin's presence, and an amazing three-way conversation took place.

Chapters 6-9 tell the story of the communications I had with Martin, through Paul, during the years that followed. Martin was aware of events in my life, and told of his passing, and why he now realised that it had been his time to go. He also described his new life in the spirititual world. There follow accounts of similar experiences by two of my friends whose husbands have also passed over.

In chapter 11 I write of my experience of bereavement. Some readers may wish to skip over this, while others may find it resonates with their own feelings or helps them to a greater understanding of what one may undergo at this difficult time.

In Part II of the book I write about mediumship and the joys and difficulties of creating a contact between those in the life beyond death and those of us on Earth. There are quotations from many of the communications which have been received over the years giving us valuable information about our loved ones and the world they now inhabit.

We are all at different stages in our understanding, and for those new to the subject, Part II will, I hope, help to explain and give a background to what is described in Part I. It is "the clay of other people's experiences and writings" which reveals "the mould into which the first pot was cast", as Jan so beautifully puts it in his foreword. The books I quote from have helped and inspired me over the years, and I hope you will feel encouraged to seek some of them out for yourself.

I am a Quaker and, in the final chapter, I describe the setting up of the Quaker Fellowship for Afterlife Studies in 2000. Martin and I were among a small group who felt that there was a need for a wider understanding and appreciation, within the Society of Friends, of the spiritual/psychic knowledge which is available to us all. I quote from some of the thinking and experiences of other founder members and tell how the group has developed and flourished over the past ten years.

*

If we go on a trip abroad we make enquiries, see our papers are in order, buy maps and guide books, perhaps even learn a new language. We know it is unwise to do anything without the necessary research. And yet most people go into the greatest journey of life … death, without *any* knowledge, even without any awareness that there is knowledge to be had. No wonder many of us are fearful.

Continuity of life is a part of natural law and its conditions are subject to it. There are no taboos on exploration and seeking knowledge in a responsible way, except those which have been placed there by human beings for their own purposes. This is what I have come to believe through my experience of life and my reading.

*

As I write, I find myself meandering off into all sorts of other thoughts; related and relevant, I hope, but possibly at times a little confusing to the reader. The reason is that I am drawing on a lifetime of interest in this subject of death and what comes after, in which I have had memorable experiences and met gifted and fascinating people. During the writing process, I realised I could use asterisks to give the freedom to leap in time, or dart off to another memory. I hope you will be willing to follow!

My main reason for writing this book is for ourselves as human beings, living the physical life, living in fear of the separation of death and our own possible obliteration. But equally it is for those who have passed over and want to tell us that they have entered an amazing new world and are able to visit us to reassure us that all is well.

There will always be loss and sadness, it is part of our human experience, but I do not believe it was ever intended that we should feel cut off from our loved ones by the event of death. Communication with them can be inspiring, uplifting, reassuring, and at the same time, matter of fact, humorous and sometimes even irritating.

Above all, the experiences I have had have convinced me that those we are close to remain "only a thought away".

Angela Howard, January 2010.

*Our wedding day. 8th October, 1976.
Outside Bardfield Quaker Meeting House.*

The poster read: "...walk cheerfully over the world, answering that of God in everyone." This is the conclusion to a letter written by George Fox (1624-1691), regarded as the founder of Quakerism. Something to live up to, we both felt.

Part I

The truest end of life, is to know the life that never ends. He that makes this his care, will find his crown at last. And he that lives to live ever, never fears dying: nor can the means be terrible to him, that heartily believes the end.

For though death be a dark passage, it leads to immortality, and that's recompense enough for the suffering of it. And yet faith lights us, even through the grave, being the evidence of things not seen.

And this is the comfort of the good, that the grave cannot hold them, and that they live as soon as they die. For death is no more than a turning of us over from time to eternity. Death, then, being the way and condition of life, we cannot love to live, if we cannot bear to die.

They that love beyond the world can never be separated by it. Death cannot kill what never dies. Nor can spirits ever be divided that love and live in the same Divine Principle, the root and record of their friendship. If absence be not death, neither is theirs.

Death is but crossing the world, as friends do the seas, they live in one another still. For they must needs be present, that love and live in that which is omnipresent. In this divine glass, they see face to face and their converse is free, as well as pure.

This is the comfort of friends, that though they may be said to die, yet their friendship and society are, in the best sense, ever present because immortal.

William Penn, 1693

Quaker Faith and Practice, The book of Christian discipline of the Yearly Meeting of the Religious Society of Friends (Quakers) in Britain. 1995, edition.

Chapter 1

Endings and beginnings

Friday, January 5th, 2007

I had being staying with friends near Maldon, Essex. My way home lay close to the cemetery where Martin is buried and I decided to visit the grave. I wanted to see the woodland burial site again and whether our silver birch tree was still alive. In the drought of the summer before I had visited once and staggered to and fro with cans of water, probably just saving its life. Two days later the rain began.

Today a pale winter sun is shining. The ground is sodden. I am driving between the graves with their conventional headstones to the woodland burial site beyond. The narrow little road dips down and then suddenly rises up ahead of me. At the crest of the hill a huge expanse of sky takes my breath away. It has been washed to a clear pale blue by the recent storms, and the clouds are strewn across it like shreds of torn muslin.

This is one of those moments that you know will be memorable. January 5th. Almost exactly three years since Martin died. It feels as if it's time to start writing the book.

The birch tree is alive and has little catkins.

*

On Thursday, 18th December, 2003, we made our second visit to Paul Lambillion for Martin to have a healing session. Paul is a spiritual counsellor and healer, who lives in Bury St. Edmunds, Suffolk.

He greeted us at the front door wearing on his head a pair of plastic reindeer horns adorned with tiny light bulbs. The horns winked at us as the bulbs flashed on and off. We didn't know it then but Martin had only three days of Earthly life left. It could have been a solemn occasion but, of course, it wasn't.

You are seldom long in Paul's company before there is laughter. Great gusts of it. The butt of his humour is usually himself. He is a genuinely compassionate and humorous man who looks for the lighter side of life and finds it. He is like everybody's idea of a favourite uncle.

When there is no chance of recovery for the physical body, healing can work to loosen the ties and free us for the transition which is called death. This, I am sure, was the case on that occasion. We returned home and Martin ate a hearty supper. That was the last day he was really himself. During the Friday and Saturday he slept a great deal, unnatural deep sleep from which it was difficult to rouse him. When he was conscious he complained of feeling sick and was beginning to lose co-ordination and to stumble around at times and fall. His speech was slurred and not always rational.

On the Saturday, I remember that there was a high wind and that I cleaned the bathroom vigorously, wondering what was happening. I also called out the doctor who said he thought the cancer might have spread to Martin's brain. I had had long practice in not thinking far ahead and, besides, I was exhausted. I simply reacted to what was happening and tried to cope. I don't remember any emotions except a deep dread of the future.

We were sleeping in separate rooms so as not to disturb each other. On Saturday night Martin was stumbling about at times and falling on his way to the bathroom. I tried to persuade him to call me for help but it didn't seem to be working. Eventually I found him lying on the floor at an awkward angle. I couldn't rouse him. I phoned my friend and next door neighbour, Margaret, and she came over with her son, who happened to be visiting her. The three of us got him back into bed. Self-preservation and a cool practicality seemed to come over me and I remember thinking that I could no longer manage and that he might have to go into hospital.

Early Sunday morning he called me and said he had a bad headache. I lay beside him on our bed and put my arms round him. He went into a deep sleep and somehow I realised he was dying. There had been an urgency about his need to find me and I knew he wanted me there to help.

I reassured him that all would be well and began to speak a meditation about letting go and going to the Light. I could tell from his breathing that he was becoming more and more deeply unconscious. All this is now a bit vague in my mind but I do remember very clearly the last words he spoke. He said "I'm sorry, I was trying to prove…" It was very slurred. I had to ask him to repeat it. He did. And on that half-sentence he went out of his Earthly life. He went out, the scientist in him feeling that the experiment he'd been engaged in had failed.

It would have been nice if he'd said goodbye, or that he loved me. But really there was no need. I knew he loved me and it wasn't goodbye. Our dialogue has continued in a different form. Thanks mainly to Paul. And I could easily supply that last, missing half sentence. He was trying to say, "I'm sorry I was trying to prove that you can recover from cancer using alternative therapies." It was a challenge he had accepted on the day he received the diagnosis.

After it was over I broke down. Margaret came again and looked after me and in due course, through the day, members of the family arrived and everyone gently carried me through the first desperate hours of my grief. But it was a grief relieved and warmed by joy. I knew Martin had entered into a new life free from pain and restriction. And it had all happened more quickly and easily than I could have hoped. It was just that suddenly we seemed separate after years of being together, and after the extra closeness of struggling, of plotting and scheming to overcome the illness. We had been yoked together day and night in the intensity of that struggle, and now he had left, and I didn't know quite where he was or what was happening to him. I just had to trust and let him go. I knew he would be in safe and loving hands, but they were other hands than mine.

Chapter 2

About us

I come of Quaker stock. As a child I was aware of a multitude of relations and was brought up with an understanding of the ramifications of both family trees, and what was meant when someone was referred to as a second cousin once removed.

My mother was Margaret Joan Headley; she was a gifted amateur pianist, particularly valued as an accompanist to singers. Her father and his brother started the printing firm of Headley Brothers in Ashford, Kent.

My father, Joseph Smith, came of an Essex farming family, and I was fortunate to grow up in a lovely home with the freedom to roam in a large garden with a pond, on which 'boats' made of oil drums and planks of wood floated or, more usually, sank. Beyond the garden were meadows, where Friesian cows grazed in summer. There were always cats and dogs to play with and I had an excitable pony whom I fell off frequently. I had two sisters, fourteen and eleven years older than me, so in my early years I was effectively an only child.

My parents met at Sidcot, the Quaker boarding school in Somerset, during the First World War. My father went straight into the Friends' Ambulance Unit at the age of 17, and served in France. He wrote to my mother who was still at the school, and she crept down to the boiler room at night to read his letters in secret!

As there were no sons in my generation to carry on running the farms, they were sold when my father died in 1971. My mother and I moved into a cottage just down the road which we called Webb's Cottage after the family who had lived there during my childhood. Later when Martin joined us here we came to realise that the name could also signify a web of connectedness, an idea which we liked very much.

*

Martin's parents were born and grew up in Northampton. His father, Sydney Leslie Howard, known as Leslie, was a rating and valuation officer until the war, first in London then, after he married in 1938, in Sale, Lancashire. His mother, Muriel Frances Wilkinson, was personal assistant to the managing director of a large department store in Northampton before her marriage. Later, as her four children (three boys and a girl) grew older, she returned to work again as a school secretary in various schools in Somerset where the family had eventually settled.

The Second World War disrupted the early years of the marriage. Muriel, with Martin, her first child, moved all round the south of England to be near Leslie: Newton Ferrers, near Plymouth, Crawley, Newhaven, Gosport.

Leslie finished the war in Buxtehude as a Lieutenant in the Royal Naval Volunteer Reserve. He was good at German, and went to Belsen as an education officer to write the formal reports. Here he met a Polish priest who was a great influence on his life, and he eventually became a Roman Catholic. Muriel remained an Anglican, and her faith and work in her local church were always important to her.

After the war Leslie took the Emergency Teacher Training programme and began a career as a music teacher, taking his

LRAM by means of a correspondence course and summer schools. He moved many times during his working life, and finally retired to Wells in Somerset. He continued to teach the cello privately for some years, and he and Muriel gained great pleasure from working as guides at Wells Cathedral. It was at this stage of their lives that I came to know them as my parents-in-law.

*

Although my childhood was idyllic, my teenage years brought an unwelcome change. I really didn't want to grow up. On top of this I was pre-occupied more and more with the important questions of life: Why are we here? Where are we going? My parents believed in a loving God in Heaven, a place where we would all be re-united with those we had loved on Earth. It was reassuring and comforting but much too vague for me. I prayed desperately for help and tried to find answers in books. My mother had books on spiritual healing – a series by Rebecca Beard, a doctor who was also a spiritual healer, books by Brother Mandus, and of course, Harry Edwards. These provided something of what I needed, and I also remember puzzling over *An Experiment With Time* by J.W. Dunne, which I must have found in the school library.

Out of step with others in my age group who were plunging into the world of parties and dances and first relationships with boys, I fell into an undiagnosed state of ill-health which I imagine was a form of depression. My worried mother was constantly taking me to the doctor to describe my latest psychosomatic symptoms. He grew very tired of me and completely failed to suggest any helpful treatment.

In spite of huge difficulties with concentration, I managed to get some GCE 'O' and 'A' levels and was eventually accepted to train as a physiotherapist at King's College Hospital, in London. I was, in reality, much more drawn to drama – writing and acting – but having failed an audition at the Central School of Speech and Drama, I decided that this was an omen and that I should do something more 'worthwhile' with my life. I was not persuaded in this by my parents, but in those days there were no Quaker role models in the theatre and I felt it would be a difficult career choice which would need a lot of courage to pursue. I was also rather alarmed by the bohemian lifestyle of some girls I knew who were going on to become actresses. I was fascinated by them but not at all sure I would fit in and feel safe in the world of the theatre.

My salvation came through psychotherapy arranged for me by my mother. I had a wonderful Jungian therapist who gradually helped me come to an understanding of myself, whereupon my energy began to return and I was able to start my training. I did eventually qualify, though I found it a struggle, and I worked as a physiotherapist in several hospitals in the UK and for a spell in Canada.

I've always found hospitals stressful places which deplete my energy, and by the time I met Martin I was working privately in the area of counselling and stress management with small groups or on a one-to-one basis.

Writing and acting have always been a much loved and inspirational part of my life. Drama revitalizes me; I have continued to find it truly re-creational.

*

My father's death in November 1971 was a huge event in my life. It happened quite suddenly one morning just as I was leaving for work. This was four years before I met Martin, when

I was in my early thirties, living with my parents and working at a local hospital. My father had been complaining of what he thought was indigestion the day before, but after breakfast that morning he suffered such severe pain that we phoned for an ambulance. He had had a coronary thrombosis in 1961, so we were aware of a heart problem, but he had been reasonably fit during the intervening years.

As I stood helplessly beside my father, and watched him collapse into unconsciousness I was aware that he might be dying. But I had the strong feeling that his personality could not disappear; could not be wiped out. He might be leaving us but he was going somewhere else; *he could not cease to exist*. He died before he reached the hospital leaving the family in shock and devastation. He was such a strong, loving man. I once again found myself asking urgent questions about the nature of life and death.

Sometime after my father's death, my mother agreed that we should become vegetarian. I had been wanting to take this step for some time. I joined the Friends' Vegetarian Society and met Grace and Terence Lane, the secretary and treasurer, who lived in nearby Chelmsford. The Lanes were frail and elderly and didn't own a car. They asked me if I would visit a FVS member they knew of who was living in sheltered accommodation in one of the local villages, and feeling rather isolated. I gathered that there was some sort of difficulty in her past regarding her Quaker connection.

When I walked into Elsie Smith's living room I saw a bright, diminutive woman sitting in front of a bookcase of vast proportions, crammed with books. Elsie provided an important step in my path. She was psychic and some of the books were written by first generation Spiritualists such as Frederic Myers. The 'shadow' in Elsie's past lay in the fact that she had been giving messages which came to her from a spiritual source in her Quaker meeting as part of her ministry. When the elders of the meeting discouraged her in this, Elsie stopped attending. I read some of the messages she had collected in an exercise book. They were beautiful and inspiring and the language used was quite unlike Elsie's usual style of speaking. I later came to know this as the phenomenon of channelling which I write more about in chapter 12.

Of course I began to borrow Elsie's books. Some of the classic Spiritualist texts I found rather heavy going. The ideas were wonderful but the style was old fashioned and convoluted. But they *existed*, and opened a new world to me. Eventually they led to a visit to the College of Psychic Studies in South Kensington, London, where I found books more to my taste such as *The Road to Immortality* by Geraldine Cummins and *Testimony of Light* by Helen Greaves, in the library and bookshop.

I continued to visit Elsie and learned much from her, particularly about synchronicity – the occurrence of events that form a meaningful pattern in life. She was full of fascinating stories, and meeting her reassured me that I was on a journey of discovery that could lead somewhere positive.

When people say there is no evidence that we survive death, I always think of the library of the College of Psychic Studies and also the library at The Arthur Findlay College, Stansted Hall, which is probably even larger. How sad it is that most people will never know that evidence of life after death abounds in these rooms. What of the effort to communicate which those writers made? Were they all liars and cheats? If so, we are accusing some of the best minds of the nineteenth and twentieth centuries of fraud. Surely, after all the thought and work which they gave to an immensely important subject (and the ridicule they often endured to bring this knowledge to us) we should at least read their books?

*

The years that followed were difficult ones. My mother became very dependent on me after my father's death, and we were both trying to care for a close family member who had a serious alcohol problem.

At the time, I was secretary of Quaker Concern for Animals, a voluntary post which I held for over 25 years, and in the summer of 1975, desperately needing a break, I booked to go on a holiday conference arranged by the Catholic Study Circle for Animal Welfare. It was being held on the campus of Aberystwyth University during what turned out to be a blisteringly hot week in July, and as I rattled across Wales, already a day late and in a train devoid of air conditioning, I was hoping against hope that everything would run smoothly at home during my absence.

I was exhausted and didn't know if I was on my head or my heels, and then, soon after I arrived on the campus, I met Martin. *He* had also been needing a break as he was in the middle of a divorce. As he was a Catholic and a member of the CSCAW, the holiday had seemed a good choice for him. He was emotionally very fragile, missing his four children desperately, and pouring out his troubles to anyone who would listen! I did listen, and although I could see that we had much in common and I felt attracted to him, by the end of the week a combination of his intensity and the heat made me desperate to put distance between us.

A few weeks later we realised we were missing each other and began to correspond. We arranged a meeting in Kew Gardens, in London, on a day of continuous, deluging rain! We dodged from one huge conservatory to the next, pretending to look at the plants, talking and talking, utterly absorbed in one another. Later, after a meal, we sat through a performance of *The*

Mousetrap, our clothes damp and clammy. How much of the play we really took in I don't know; our heads and hearts were in a whirl, because we both knew that a real relationship could be beginning.

Martin wrote: "We thought alike and exchanged our minds before our hearts."

*

Martin understood and accepted my family responsibilities in a way I had thought no potential husband ever could or would. We both had complicated lives but we agreed to share everything, good, bad and downright ghastly. And we did. For me our meeting was a miracle, and I think for him also.

In that first year, he was working in Croydon and living in a tiny bedsitter. We exchanged long letters, sometimes daily, and spent weekends together, beginning a dialogue which was to continue until the day he died. He was a planning officer working in local government when we met and for the last twenty years of his professional life, from 1980, he worked from home as a planning consultant, and so we were together morning, noon and night.

Meeting Martin was like re-discovering an old friend. It was as if we were united at the level of the soul but had been temporarily apart. We didn't always have a great deal to say to each other on an everyday level; in fact both of us were basically loners, but what we did have was a shared interest in spiritual and philosophical matters and in trying to put our understanding into practice. All through our lives both of us had been asking "what's the purpose of it all?" We had found ourselves to be out of step with most of humanity, and were both unhappy as a result.

When he began visiting me Martin discovered my books! Books which as a Roman Catholic he had not been allowed to read because they were on the proscribed list – something I'd never heard of. He fell upon them avidly. And over the years together we both added to them, so that today the collection is large. Buying books was probably our greatest extravagance!

We were married a year later, in October '76, at the Quaker Meeting House in the charming north Essex village of Great Bardfield. This Meeting House which I have attended all my life has a beautiful atmosphere, and feels like a second home to me. Many of my Smith ancestors are buried in the burial ground there.

*

Martin's divorce and re-marriage put him in a difficult position. He had grown up an Anglican but had become a Catholic before his first marriage, and had married in church. We both started attending the Catholic church in Great Bardfield when he visited me at weekends, and after the service would take a short walk through the village to the Meeting House. The timing fitted well and it had been a happy combination, the Catholic service giving us much to think about (and sometimes minister about), in the quiet hour that followed. As a single man he was accepted by the congregation at the Great Bardfield church; at least no questions were asked. However, when we married it was a very different matter, and he sadly found himself given the cold shoulder. As divorce is not accepted by the Catholic Church, his marriage to me was considered bigamous.

So Martin gradually found himself more at home in the Society of Friends. He wrote, "…my faith in humanity had taken a few knocks and in many respects I was already excommunicated from the R.C. Church. But then the openness and free-thinking of Quakers caught the imagination, and not just fleetingly.

"If such a group of well meaning people could respect each other and everyone outside as well, why have any mind-restricting dogma? Gradually the ties of imposed belief were broken: *I was free to think.*"

*

We began our married life in a flat in Croydon, but quite soon Martin managed to get a job in Essex and we joined my mother at the cottage. As the years went by, circumstances changed around us, problems lessened and an easier pattern of life gradually evolved. My mother died in 1983, and though I missed her terribly I knew that for some time she had been ready to join my father and the rest of the family. It also became easier for us to have Martin's children and other visitors to stay.

As a birthright Quaker I would find it difficult to think of myself as anything else; and yet I was perpetually on a search. We explored the New Age ideas that were emerging at that time, reading voraciously and going to all the conferences that we could. It was fascinating and we were happily absorbing information like a couple of sponges. Suddenly we seemed in tune with the times we were living in, as if we had been waiting all our lives for them to happen.

Martin always had tremendous energy and did things with zest and enthusiasm. He loved experimenting. From the 'pinhole glasses' (pairs of which he passed on to many friends) he used to strengthen his eyes, to the strange pipes coming out of the septic tank which were supposed to irrigate the vegetable garden but suffered blockages and smelt badly in hot weather, the stranger the idea the better he liked it - provided it made sense to him. And I loved him for this. It made life exciting and his was the kind of mind which often produces wonderful new inventions.

At one course we attended he was encouraged to develop his gift as a healer, and over the years, trained, and became a healer member of Friends' Fellowship of Healing. He was also fascinated by the international language, Esperanto, and quickly became proficient in it, beginning a correspondence with Esperantists in Poland, where the language originated, and making many friends there.

Over the years, we had Polish visitors to stay at the cottage, and Martin would spend a month in the summer visiting Polish friends and giving healing. In those days conditions under the Communist regime made life extremely difficult and people were grateful for any help, particularly with their health problems. He would set off for Poland armed with large amounts of Potter's passiflora tablets which can help with sleeping problems, and acidosis tablets which aid digestion, to distribute to his friends!

He also joined the Peace Tax Campaign which was started by those who refuse to pay the percentage of their income tax which would be used by the government for the purposes of war. On two consecutive summers he set off on his bicycle to travel the length and breadth of England giving talks at Quaker Meeting Houses and public halls. I would meet up with him at certain strategic points to exchange dirty laundry for clean, as he was never in one place long enough for his washing to dry. *I* had the luxury of travelling by car!

Just remembering and listing all the things Martin did makes me feel tired! The cottage was a hive of activity as he was also working for the Quaker Esperanto Society, and editing and printing booklets, using his computer. The printer often worked away all night, so it seemed as if the industry never stopped. I think you will get the picture!

I tried to help him to keep his days manageable! At times I had to put a brake on his more way-out enthusiasms and help him re-organise his life. He never really believed that there are only twenty-four hours in a day and so, when I saw him getting short-tempered and stressed, I would suggest we sat down with a cup of tea, looked at his priorities, and tried to prune some of the jobs and projects he had acquired.

*

Life was good. Especially after 1998 when Martin decided to retire early from his planning consultancy because of increasing deafness and disillusion with bureaucracy. He had been attending pottery classes once a week for about ten years and it had become a passion he dreamed of pursuing.

With the help of an unexpected windfall from a family trust we were able to make the dream a reality. The cottage only has two decent sized bedrooms and it had always been difficult to accommodate visitors, so Martin designed and oversaw the construction of a small building to house a pottery on the ground floor, and a double bedroom above. By the late summer of '98 there it was in the garden, standing pristine and ready, its steeply pitched tile roof echoing that of the cottage.

What an exciting time this was. Martin bought a kiln and two wheels and later a pug mill to take the hard labour out of preparing the clay. Then there was all the shelving to put up and the tools to find. Finally the clay itself arrived in huge slabs that were brown and glistening and full of promise. Martin was a very happy shopper and what he managed to squirrel away in his little bit of heaven was quite amazing as I came to discover when only six years later I had to dismantle it all.

Apart from making his own pottery, Martin taught one or

two students the basic skills, and also gave 'pottery parties'. A group of up to six children would arrive, accompanied by one or two parents, usually as a birthday treat for one of them, and spend two hours modelling and making coil pots. The results would be fired and ready for collection at a later date. It was delightful to see the children so totally absorbed in producing imaginative work, but when they had finished and came rushing out into the garden, their pent-up energy would send them flying in all directions and I worried someone would finish up in the pond!

Packing and firing the kiln was an important part of Martin's life and he became tense and nervous at these times so that I kept out of his way. I was always with him when he opened the kiln however, because it was so exciting to see the pottery come out. Like two children on Christmas morning we couldn't wait! As the heavy door swung slowly open, the heat would come pouring out and envelop us! I loved to watch Martin's face as he carefully lifted out each piece. Our hearts would go up and down like yo-yos, and we would gasp and groan in quick succession. Some pieces which had taken him hours and hours to make would be cracked or blown, some would have completely changed colour, some would be perfect. Sometimes there would be a piece which was a different colour from what he had intended but actually looked wonderful. I would run my eye greedily over each piece, trying to decide how many of the best I could reasonably filch for the cottage!

Another thing Martin loved to do was to put his wheel and all his equipment into a trailer and drive off to set up at a fête or fair. He would offer children and adults the chance to throw a pot, and a little crowd always gathered around him, waiting for a turn or just watching in fascination. He was good at explaining and demonstrating, and had a gift for inspiring people of all ages to develop a love for the craft.

Visitors to the cottage would get out of their cars, look around, listen to the silence for a moment or two, take a deep breath, and often just say one word, 'idyllic'. A cat might then appear on cue to pose artistically and complete the scene. We were both fifty-nine, the dream could have continued for another twenty years. But, of course, it didn't.

Chapter 3

A journey with cancer

Martin virtually ignored the early signs of a prostate problem. He wouldn't see a doctor. He believed in knowing one's own body and using alternative therapies, but deep down I think that like most of humanity he just didn't think it could happen to him. He felt fit and strong. He had a good diet with lots of home-grown vegetables, and he lived healthily, why should he be ill? When he was diagnosed with cancer he made every effort to get well through the use of alternative therapies and other systems of self-healing.

Tuesday, 15th October 2002, was the last reasonably normal day of our married life; a day when the future seemed to stretch before us in much the same way as the past lay stretched behind. On the 16th Martin had an appointment at the local hospital to hear the results of a biopsy and CT scan. I thought it was suspicious that he had been given a scan so quickly after the biopsy, and then called back to hear the results at the hospital rather than getting them from his GP. I am more familiar with hospital procedures than he was, and also more of a pessimist.

In the morning, like any typical retired couple, we took a trip to a nearby garden centre and had lunch in the restaurant there. Then to the hospital where the bombshell was dropped. Martin had an aggressive form of prostate cancer which had already spread to the surrounding bone. No treatment was offered except some hormone tablets.

The news followed a summer of waiting and indecision. First I had had to nag him to see a doctor, then there had been a certain amount of delay and incompetence on the part of the NHS. (The sort of thing most of us are sadly familiar with.) Nothing had moved swiftly until the biopsy was examined.

Speechless, we sat in the pharmacy waiting for the pills to be dispensed. Afterwards we both remembered the small pile of earth on the carpet which had spilled out of a plant pot, and the half-empty plastic coffee cup beside it. A strange little snapshot etched on two completely numb and uncomprehending brains.

I remember walking behind Martin along a narrow path to the car park. He looked so reassuringly solid; surely he couldn't be going to die? Because I couldn't imagine life without him the future seemed suddenly to have collapsed into a void.

We just wanted to get home. I can't remember what we said on the fifteen-mile drive, but we were met outside the cottage by Margaret, our friend who lived next door. She had been looking out for the car, well aware of the possibility of bad news. Her response was extraordinary and made me gasp. "Well, what are you going to do now?" she asked, briskly.

It was the perfect thing to say to Martin who was always active and with a plan in mind. I remember going indoors and sitting in a chair and shaking uncontrollably. For a short while Martin was tearful and disbelieving: it was very uncharacteristic. He rang one of his brothers and one of his sons, and then as the first shock started to wear off he began to formulate a way of defeating the cancer through a combination of alternative therapies. We had read about miraculous cures and he became determined that this was what he was going to achieve. He felt well in himself, and strong, and had so much to live for. "I'm not going anywhere," was what he often said in those early days.

I always knew that Martin wanted to deal with his life in his own way, and I had to respect this. He was that sort of person. The only real row we had during his illness was when he told me not to interfere so much. And I never knew him to have a shred of self pity during the whole of the fourteen months that were left to him. Sometimes he was quiet and went within himself, but nearly always he was cheerful and positive, and if he suffered a bout of pain was quickly back to his old self once it was alleviated. But he did try to persuade other men to visit the doctor at an earlier stage than he had.

*

At this time we shared our home with two cats of rather spiky disposition. One in particular, a brindled lady whom we had acquired from the RSPCA, expressed her feelings, if not fed the instant she required it, by flattening back her ears in temper and ripping the stair carpet. She also ripped visitors if they were inclined to stroke her in the wrong way. I always had sticking plaster ready in those days and often needed it. Despite my dire warnings, venturesome new-comers to our home would make the wrong move with Meg and the claws would go in. And sometimes the teeth as well. We put it down to ill-treatment in the past. We took her on as a challenge, well aware of her reputation, and worked on her over the years, but although she settled down and her social skills improved, she was never a cat to be trifled with. Meg is probably no longer on this Earth: she disappeared suddenly and without trace in May 2005.

Our other cat, Prue, is a green-eyed beauty with long dark fur and a tail like a feather boa. She is not prone to using her claws like Meg, but she is shy and fearful and if she does deign to sit on your lap, the slightest movement will upset her and she'll swiftly leave again. So neither of our cats was what you might call a cosy, lap cat, a contented radiator of love. And that was what Martin really wanted and needed, and he would often say so. And then Nova arrived in our lives.

Some neighbours, in their eighties and not feeling able to cope with caring for an animal, found a cat haunting their backdoor step. She was in good condition and didn't seem to have been living rough; yet she obviously couldn't find her way home. They fed her for a week but didn't let her inside. Instead, as October turned to November, and all efforts to find her owner failed, they phoned us, knowing we had a fondness for cats.

Martin went round to see her and returned wreathed in smiles. He loved animals and would always get down on his hands and knees to join the smaller ones in their own world. Nova (she had no name that we knew of then, of course) had somehow finished up draped around his neck. She was the perfect cat and we had to give her a home.

She arrived and settled in quickly. She is a tabby with flares of ginger in her coat. She was fully grown and had, still has, a tummy like a little Buddha. We thought she might be going to have kittens at first, but no, she'd been spayed, the vet said. She never seems very interested in food but her waist measurement remains impressive.

The name Nova came from the month she moved in with us, and from 'nova', the Esperanto word for new. We felt she must have arrived in the village in a delivery lorry or van. She is very curious and will jump into, and onto, things before she's really thought the matter through. In many ways she has the confident eagerness of a dog.

Early in her life here, she followed Meg through a skylight and onto the roof, and then fell off it, (or was she pushed?) She took several days to fully recover from her crash landing.

But the great thing about her is her love for human company. She was Martin's purring companion throughout his illness and she still sleeps on my bed at night and is around me all day. She is perfection and, although I am sad for her former owner, I do feel that maybe she was sent to help us at a very difficult time in our lives.

*

We always did what we could to avoid exploiting animals in our daily lives although we didn't go as far as many of our vegan friends. We used alternative therapies because we felt they are gentler and more natural, and also because orthodox medicine is firmly rooted in animal experimentation.

Martin took tablets to relieve pain during the last six months of his life, but otherwise depended on a variety of alternative therapies. He was in deep shock when he accepted the hormone tablets and soon rejected them, partly because he didn't like their side effects. If any other orthodox treatment had been offered he would probably have rejected that too. How I would have felt about this I really don't know. When life-threatening illness comes to us we all tend to clutch at whatever is available. We are human and vulnerable and we have to make compromises with our principles in this imperfect world. This is especially so when we have commitments to young children, or other family members, or our work, or are burdened financially. Martin was free of all these, and he always believed that I am strong enough to stand on my own.

As it was, nothing further was offered by the hospital and as he gradually adjusted to his situation, he started on a programme of self-healing with the support of many therapists. I do not propose to go into detail on the daily regime he used. Clearly it did not heal the cancer. It did, however, give him a very good quality of life for much of the remaining time he had left. Although he was already using a catheter to pass urine, he felt extremely well during the first months. He had tremendous hope and a positive outlook, and was keen to experiment and discover, using his own body on which to conduct research. What was clear from the outset, and it was typical of him, was that he wanted to take control and be responsible.

*

At some point in the early nineteen-nineties, Martin and I gave a talk about our lives to Bardfield Quaker Meeting. We wrote it as a dialogue. It was part of a programme which aimed at helping Friends get to know one another at greater depth.

What follows is the conclusion to Martin's section. It was written at a time when the world was opening up to him through Esperanto and the internet, and it shows that although he loved his life, his spirit was that of the explorer in the widest sense. Martin's use of capital letters was always quite individual. I have not changed anything he wrote – although I have been tempted!

Life with Angela and the three cats, the garden, the wild area, the cottage itself, is idyllic. Coming to Meeting on Sundays, going off on the tandem together, trying to dovetail our lives together should be total bliss. And yet ...there is always the feeling that there is something out there waiting, pulling me toward itself; some new change, new experience before this round finishes. Perhaps I will not always remain a quaker and a spiritualist.

For now I am prepared to just listen to what life is trying to tell me... After a lifetime when I was not able to adequately communicate because of stuttering, when my ideas were regarded as quite silly by my peers, when I could not communicate outside my own country, I now communicate easily with people all over the world.

These people over the water actually listen to me, ask questions and really want to know the answers. I go to Poland each year and have trouble acclimatising when I come back. I freely communicate there about quakerism and other religions, health and healing, politics, all kinds of ideas, and that is not just the effect of the vodka! Now I even communicate, just a little, in Polish, publish all kinds of leaflets about animal welfare, Esperanto plays, quaker material in three languages.

My communication with myself, with the god within and the energies without has grown stronger, more sure of itself ...and yet, the more that feeling grows, the more I realise that there are many more lives to come, many more experiences, many more thoughts that my present poorly evolved mind is not able to contemplate. I am looking forward to coming back ... next time. Will we meet again?

*

A vivid memory comes back to me. It is ten months since Martin's cancer was diagnosed. I am sitting on a lawn on a July evening listening to music. Above me a huge velvety sky is darkening into night and beginning to twinkle with stars. It is one of those times you wish will never end.

The summer of 2003 is hot and dry but the temperature now is perfection. I am one of a group of patients and their supporters/carers, and we are on a five day course at the Bristol Cancer Help Centre. We are receiving the kind of imaginative loving care for all our needs that I wish everyone suffering from cancer and their loved ones could experience.

We are helped to understand the healing properties of foods, to deal with our negative emotions and to accept possible futures through meditation and art work. We have a chance to talk to doctors who are prepared to explain and listen and help each one of us to an individual plan of treatment which includes both the orthodox and alternative, or complementary, approach. We receive healing and massage (a bit of a sticky process in this weather) and counselling. At times the patients meet together as a separate group, as do the carers. Martin and I spend a lot of time in the chapel in which all the world faiths are represented. Mostly we each choose to go on our own, sometimes in the middle of the night as the heat is making sleep difficult, and we find our small twin-bedded room claustrophobic.

Everyone present is struggling in some way or another with their present life, and with fears about what the future may hold. Five people have come on their own, and there are eight of us in pairs. There is a young, newly married couple very much in love, the wife with the cancer, completely unable to contemplate life without each other. There is a mother and daughter from Scotland, the daughter with the cancer. I talk a lot with the mother who is exhausted and drained. There is also a daughter of seventeen who has come as a carer for her mother – at times the whole situation becomes too much for her and she misses sessions, appearing a bit bolshy. The rest of us understand and sympathise. Relationships are forming within the group. Everyone feels for everyone else and the emotional temperature is high, with explosions of anger and tears but also times of deep healing and revelation.

The programme does not suit everyone. There are upset tummies because the vegetarian whole food diet is new to some people. (Escapees go out to search for chips!) One man from a military family and a conventional background says he has only really come to learn about the diet. He finds it difficult to show his feelings in the way we are being encouraged to do, and the meditation sessions feel alien to him. He leaves before the end of the course, but admits he has much to think about.

Martin is in his element. For the first time he talks to a doctor who understands him and everything he is trying to do. How completely different from the hospital experience! He is in quite a lot of pain at times but we walk to the Bristol Suspension Bridge and cross it, gazing down into the chasm beneath. One evening he manages to dance, but regrets it later.

A highlight of the visit is playing in the orchestra! Thirteen of us on a variety of instruments are somehow co-ordinated by an experienced conductor so that we are able to give an impromptu concert. It's a bit of a miracle. We manage to play more or less together and make a sound that is passable, even inspiring. It feels great just to let off steam and have fun, and for a few moments everything else is forgotten.

Martin, in his deafness, discovers the joys of the xylophone. A good musician on the organ and piano, he quickly learns enough to hammer away and produce a version of the *Ode to Joy* from Beethoven's ninth symphony which is the centre piece of the performance. He *feels* the music through the vibration of the keys and just loves this new sensation!

*

Another inspirational place along the trail is the Cambridge Cancer Help Centre. It is an hour's drive from the cottage and we start to visit regularly. We receive loving support and healing, and Martin begins counselling in earnest to help him with the emotional side of his life. I am so glad he is at last willing to do this as I feel it is crucial.

*

Another memory from that year. It is a warm day in early October. I am standing on a wide pavement in the centre of the modern part of Tunbridge Wells; Martin alongside. The town is divided into two, the new part with the typical chain stores and traffic jams, and the elegant eighteenth-century spa town known as The Pantiles, which has been receiving visitors, many of them royal, since the discovery of the Chalybeate Spring in 1606.

Our visit is not connected with the healing waters of the Spring. We have arrived for Martin's treatment at the Liongate Clinic. We have settled into the little flat provided for visitors and are now exploring. The day is full of sunshine, people, colour, noise. Life. Suddenly my heart lifts and I think, irrationally, Holiday! We have had weeks at home in the quiet and beauty of the cottage and garden with rather too much time to think about illness. Now, suddenly, I glimpse another world and remember the old days when we were both fit and well and in a new place sniffing the air and drinking in the atmosphere.

"Oh, I'd like to go to that!" I say, excitedly, pointing out a poster for a production of *Fiddler on the Roof*. I look round for more delights, distractions. And then I become conscious of Martin standing quietly beside me, and read his face. And I know we have to go back to the Clinic because he is in pain. How could I have forgotten?

*

The Liongate Clinic *is* the Austrian doctor, Fritz Schellander. Spare of frame, never still for long, he is a pioneer, a man with a mission. Gentle and intense and penetratingly intelligent, as he sets up the Laetrile B17 drips in the morning, he is quite likely to be asked by one of his lady receptionists if he will fix a blocked drain. And he won't mind a bit or think that the job is beneath him. Drips, drains, it's all the same to Dr. Fritz. Something that needs to be done to keep the world and people's lives running smoothly.

The Clinic offered an 'integrated approach to the treatment of cancer'. On the first day we had a long consultation with Dr. Fritz who believes that patients should be 'active participants in the treatment'. The brochure says they are 'encouraged to ask questions, to learn about themselves and their illness and will be helped to explore different treatment options'.

There were other therapists offering treatment in the many rooms of this sprawling Georgian house. Dr. Fritz planned the programme for each patient, the central core of the daily sessions being 'The Drip' which could take several hours to pass into the system. The patients sat in comfortable chairs around a ground-floor room attached to their bags of fluid. Martin, with a captive audience, was in his element. I think he got almost as much from the chat as the treatment. If he could find someone to talk to about philosophy, spirituality, the latest book he had read, unorthodox cancer cures, Esperanto, pottery, he was well away. I would come to meet him at the end of the treatment and find him animated and with his face wreathed in smiles. Possibly some of his audience were exhausted. I used to tell them they could shut him up if they wanted, and he would laughingly agree. I was delighted to see him so happy. However, Dr. Fritz warned that Martin gave out too much of himself. He had an aggressive form of cancer and needed to use his resources for his own healing. I think he tried to quieten down and read his book rather than chat, but it was a bit like asking the sun not to shine!

The Liongate Clinic is no longer functioning. We knew that it had financial problems and that Dr Fritz was on the point of exhaustion and nearing the age when most people think of retirement. When I looked at the website recently I wasn't surprised to find that it had closed. But I was saddened. He is a wonderful man and thankfully he continues to give consultations elsewhere in this country.

Martin went to "the dear Liongate", as he called it, three days a week for seven weeks through the autumn of 2003, and we were planning more visits after Christmas. He later said in a communication through Paul that the vitamin B17 did help.

For his birthday in November I bought him a xylophone. He loved it and was just starting to learn to play it. After his death, Margaret took it to Bristol when she was passing through on a trip somewhere and so it joined the other instruments at the Cancer Help Centre. That was what Martin would have wanted.

*

Martin's energy and love of life continued almost until his dying day. He tackled his illness as a challenge and thank goodness he did. He was reading new books and having new thoughts until the week before he died. He sent copies of his latest find, *Conversations with God* by Neale Donald Walsch, to his nearest and dearest, accompanied by an enthusiastic letter setting out his plans for the New Year.

When he came to sign the copies of his Christmas letter, typed in mid-December, he told me he was having difficulty writing his signature. Typically, he was far more optimistic than his actual physical state gave him reason to be. Maybe his spirit was already beginning to disconnect so that it could soon fly free.

To all dear friends and relations at Christmas 2003
and New Year
A REALLY HAPPY AND JOYFUL CHRISTMAS
AND NEW YEAR TO YOU ALL

An edited part of the letter/article I had printed in our local Quaker magazine will probably tell you all the main news and supply information as to just where I, or my mind, actually is at the moment. I managed to get rid of the editorship of this magazine and several other printing and publishing matters during the year so that I can spend time on my own healing process. I have also not been doing much pottery. But that is due to become operational again in the New Year. Healing is progressing and I should be potting, gardening, playing the xylophone etc. sometime in the Spring.

For over a year now I have been feeling my unorthodox way through prostate and bone cancer. It has given me time to love and care for myself, aided all the time of course by Angela. We don't often have the opportunity to spend time on ourselves. I have read a lot of books during that year. I now know a lot about cancer from books, experience and the net. But four books, of a more spiritual nature have also spoken deeply to me and they may do something for you as well.

The Endorphin Effect *by William Bloom. In every living cell there are endorphins which give us pleasure and take away pain. They are there for our use. A loving God within?*

The Field *by Lynne McTaggart. Every living cell is a hologram of all the knowledge of the world and probably beyond. The totality of God within everyone so that we can never be separated?*

Tracks in the Psychic Wilderness *by Dale E. Graff, former director of Project Stargate. You may think it odd for a Quaker pacifist to be reading a book by someone like Dale who was so involved with remote viewing of what the Russians were up to during the cold war. But through his research and experiences of remote viewing he has created a situation where war between super powers can never happen again, because each side can 'see' what the other is doing.*

The New Revelations *by Neale Donald Walsch. This is the latest in his wonderful books of Conversations with God. It includes 5 fallacies about God; 5 about Life: 5 Steps to Peace and finally the 9 Revelations which can change our world forever. (I use it for my personal seasonal card this year.) This book, in my opinion, will be central to our spiritual lives in this the third millennium. It may well sit on our central table in Quaker Meetings alongside* The Bible, Koran, Bhagavad-Gita, *and our* Quaker Faith and Practice. *It may well become more important than those!*

Heresy I hear you cry! I cried while reading almost every page. It so spoke, no it shouted, to my spiritual condition and that of the world around us.

I have given it as my main present this year, or the teens' or children's versions, where appropriate. That may seem odd to you, but I take the view that this season, whether we call it Christmas, Yule, New Year or some other title, depending on our religious upbringing, or none, deserves the best from me to you.

All the very best to you for this winter season and the year to follow.

Chapter 4

A Green burial

Martin died on December 21st, and I continued to write my diary every day: I found it essential to do so.

Monday, December 22nd, 2003

I have to find a new way to irradiate the cottage somehow. To pass on the love. I hope M. will return but at the moment I can only see him leaving with the funeral directors in their big vehicle. They came at 6 pm last night and were nice, one very young. I think I will put a potter's thumb (a tool) in the coffin. He is going to wear his green track suit.

His body was still so fit and strong in many ways with years of useful physical life left. It seems a terrible waste. I know there are other ways of looking at it all. I wanted him here for another 20 years – if I'm to last that long. Nancy (a friend) wrote that when Humfrey died she knew she would still have happiness and contentment in the future but the magic was gone. That is it at the moment. The magic has gone from the cottage.

*

There were different sounds around me now - other voices. A change in gear. Activity, but to a different end. Eventually there emerged the need to plan. It was Christmas. Everything was about to shut down and yet somehow there was a funeral to arrange.

I got up. I did things. Necessary things. In a daze. Often I collapsed on my bed - for hours. It was my refuge. I completely understood the phrase 'prostrate with grief'. Being in an upright position required tremendous effort. Grief is tiring. No, utterly exhausting. And I felt intense physical pain in my spine and the surrounding muscles. A burning ache that could not be eased.

When I was a physiotherapy student in the 1960s, the Second World War was still a recent memory. One of my patients told me how he had fought in the battle of El Alamein. He fired a machine gun repeatedly, hour after hour. There is a bed of rock under the desert sand, and the vibration of the guns actually cracked at least one of the metatarsal bones in his feet. It was not until after the battle that he was aware of any pain.

Somehow in a crisis you keep going. Once the crisis is over the body shrieks its agony. No one had warned me about the physical pain which seemed to merge with the emotional pain, like different sections of the same orchestra. Body and mind. Mind and body.

*

I am aware of concentric rings of people around me. Family and close friends. The people I see or speak to less often; acquaintances, neighbours, Martin's work colleagues; people who live at a distance and are contacting with Christmas cards. Now the sympathy cards are pouring in to join the daily flow of Christmas cards. Cheery Christmas cards to 'Martin and Angela', tumble into the cottage alongside sympathy cards to 'Angela'. The incongruity of it all. The confusion and crossed wires.

Just opening and reading the words requires energy. But some of the lovely messages uplift and are comforting.

The phone. I am endlessly on the phone. I prop myself up on cushions and shift the phone from one hand to the other, almost keeling over with tiredness. Everyone reacts to the news powerfully and individually. Reactions to death are strong and each person brings their own baggage and point of view. Even if not expressed, the emotion in the silences is almost palpable.

There's a great deal of shock. Disbelief. People have been receiving Martin's Christmas Letter which radiates a strange and perhaps unrealistic vitality and speaks of all his plans. And now..! About turn.

They have to understand how it was. They have to be taken through the last hours. Perhaps the last weeks and months. Description. Explanation. Consolation. The conversation has to take place with due weight and dignity, even when repeated time and again. And plans! When, where, and what is happening?

It is a blessing when other close members of the family make and receive the phone calls. And they do. And I like to listen to them. I like to hear the facts repeated over and over again by kindly voices. It helps the reality to sink in.

When other people are missing Martin I feel close to them and to him. Mike is missing his Dad. And he's so like Martin that when I see him and hear his voice the familiarity is like a stab of joy and pain at one and the same time.

He and Becky (my niece) are like a pair of strong wings on each side of me. They carry me forward and they also enfold and buffer me from the world. Mike *knows* Martin would want a Green burial, which of course he would. I had felt incapable of finding a site and making the arrangements in the available time – before everything closes down for Christmas. Mike simply looks on the internet and in no time we have decided on a site at Maldon and are whooshing off to look at it in Mike's car.

At the corner of the cemetery is a little Victorian chapel. The man showing us round says it is hardly ever used but, yes, of course, we may use it. We push open the heavy door to be met by the barest of essential furniture; a table, some benches, a strong smell of damp and, parked in the centre, a little handcart, a bier. I gaze at the bier, enthralled. "Could we decorate it?" The kindly reply is that we may do as we like.

The site for the grave is near a pond and a willow tree in a rough grassy area beyond the conventional cemetery. Many others have already been buried here so much of the earth is disturbed and tussocky. It is natural and simple. The sound of the traffic on the Maldon bypass is the only drawback and we make our decision there and then.

We drive into the town to find an old coaching inn which has been recommended to Becky. It is dark and full of creaking timber and polished brass; very atmospheric and obviously the scene of many rites of passage over the years. We order a warming array of food and drink to greet the funeral party and our order is taken with a quiet understanding of our needs. *Of course* we must have mulled wine when we arrive, and there will be flasks of hot coffee and plates of this and that which sound delicious. It will all be laid out in an upper room which is a little dim and dusty but somehow very welcoming.

I can hardly believe how everything has fallen into place. What a relief! We whoosh home and I collapse again.

The arrangements continue. Becky has everything under control and is writing list upon list. Mike is emailing maps and instructions to everyone who needs them. There are voices in the house, on the phone, at the door. I realise that it would all happen now even if I didn't lift another finger. The load is spread. I am so blessed.

Wednesday, December 31st

The funeral is over, and I think, triumphant. I had a rather rocky start to the day as the cottage seemed full of people and somewhat chaotic. Becky has been absolutely fantastic but she did seem to keep asking me how I wanted the swags made for the corners of the bier until I began to lose patience and snapped at her. So I went off to Braintree and visited Janet (our funeral director), who talked to me kindly and showed me the coffin which was wonderful – a mega picnic hamper of woven willow. I know Martin is so happy about it. I took with me some photos of his children when they were little and a pottery tool, and Janet said she would put them inside.

I went to the Co-op and had tea and a fruit scone (kindly warmed for me). Fortified, I went back to the cottage and retired upstairs having found that Bobs (another niece) had arrived and made beautiful swags. (She's a theatre director and used to making props.) Big relief. Exactly as I'd pictured them. Jasmine, variegated holly, lavender, rosemary. Gold and yellow ribbon. Lunch was happening in the kitchen but I was mostly upstairs.

Set off for Maldon with Becky and, my friend, Beryl, feeling ill and flat. Things got better. We were able to move straight in and decorate the chapel with a large bunch of flowers in the blue and mauve pot Martin loved, and little jars with night-lights inside and paper dragonflies attached. Huge difficulty lighting all the night-lights with the tapers.

Everyone arriving. Installed Peter (Martin's brother) in a corner with the tape recorder. Lovely supportive hugs. Hearse arrived. Heart stopping moment. Coffin was beautifully decorated with freesias, gypsophila, tiny daffodils and lots more.

Heart rose. Party outside, led by Claudie, were decorating the bier with a wonderful rope of ivy to stretch all around the coffin. Swags looking fantastic.

Inside Adiemus, *music by Karl Jenkins, is playing. Jacky arrives complete with her largest ear rings – Jacky's ear rings always much admired by Martin. Bliss. Peter puts on* Ode to Joy *and the door opens and the flowery coffin comes in on a triumphant burst of music and with a shaft of light. Felt absolutely radiant and that something enormous had been achieved.*

It was a meeting based on Quaker silence with many people speaking their touching memories of him, or reciting poetry. I felt abnormally cheerful because, after all the planning and worry, here we all were, and it was all happening. And I felt it was just as Martin would have wanted.

We went outside into the gathering dusk to The hills are alive with the sound of music. *Martin had watched the film many times and was a devoted fan of Julie Andrews. The bier was pushed along a bumpy path and through a small wood to the site of the grave. The little glowing dragonfly night-lights we had made bobbed along in the hands of children and adults. It was all very unusual and genuine, a real do-it-yourself funeral incorporating things which were important to Martin.*

The 'getting it right' is so important: to be able to lay someone's body to rest in a way that feels personal to them. It does help the pain of loss to carry out the rituals associated with death in an ordered and appropriate way.

Family and friends gave such support. Tim played his guitar and I banged a drum. We chanted Earth my body, water my blood, air my breath and fire my spirit. *It kept us all together and gave us power. At the grave Peter recited a poem by Anne Brontë and then we had a final poem from Tim which he had written for Martin.*

Buster began to fill in the grave using his special copper tools and others took a turn when offered the chance. Eventually we left his body there with the earth, flowers and greenery heaped around it. We entwined arms and slowly returned to the world. It had rained solidly all day but for the past hour or so the rain had held off and we were dry except for our feet.

Back at the Blue Boar a fabulous feast awaited us. It was a good time to relax and talk.

*

3rd *January, 2004*

I took Beryl home on New Year's Day and then came back to the empty house to begin living on my own. Actually found the atmosphere beautiful. Sat on the sofa and felt that it was all embracing. Have not had definite contact from Martin except a time when he seemed to be in the bedroom, but just a (sense of) warmth.

I'm talking to him in the early mornings. Telling him what I'm doing during the day. Teasing him a bit. I've found a lovely picture of him under a flowering tree. I hope I'll see him like that one day.

I have some sad moments but feel quite strong. People seem surprised at me. I have to show that what we believe makes a difference – and it does. I have to concentrate on the fact that he is free of pain and probably having good experiences – certainly challenging. Paul Lambillion has phoned and I hope to see him soon.

Chapter 5

In the bleak mid-winter

In the January of 2004, I was standing shakily on completely new territory. From the quiet of the cottage I gazed across Martin's vegetable garden at the dark windows of the pottery. It was cold and empty of life. What use could it be now? Perhaps it could still function in the way it was intended? Perhaps I could find a potter who would like to rent it? The idea of advertising and interviewing filled me with dread. I shelved it.

I realise now that I have always devised strategies to avoid falling again into depression. I could easily have become depressed then, as I had been in my teenage years. I braced myself and continued tidying the cottage. My goodness, Martin had accumulated some stuff. In his office there were surfaces that hadn't seen the light of day for ... months, years! And the cupboards bulged. And the garden was full of machinery which I knew I would never use. The sight of it made me groan inwardly, as I imagined it rotting and rusting. But I wasn't going to let that happen.

It was part of the process of mourning and recovery that I found good homes for as many of his possessions as I could. And I discovered that if I moved slowly and followed up leads, things gradually happened. Ways opened. People appeared. I found a good use for his hearing aids through a small charity. Someone even wanted the project he had struggled with as the final part of his membership of the Royal Town Planning Institute examinations because it had relevance to the re-opening of old quarries in Somerset. The company that had sold him his large compost shredder took it back again at a good price, and a builder friend found a buyer for a concrete mixer. In the process of all this I was meeting interesting, kindly people and my faith in life and normality was being gradually restored. I was learning to function as a single person.

I was still running on Martin's energy as I expressed it to myself. I was writing articles about him for the parish magazine and the local paper and talking, still talking to those who had only just found out about his death. He had been so alive and positive, people found it hard to comprehend what had happened. Even in his last months his brain had been active and his suffering largely hidden behind a cheerful smile. When he was clothed there was no visible sign of anything wrong except that he had lost weight and had a rather pale, transparent look.

There were also email friends, 'chat' room friends, websites. I am an internet innocent. I didn't understand the way things work 'up in the sky' or 'out there', as I think of it. He did, and there seemed to be many, many ramifications to his areas of contact. The world of pottery, the world of Esperanto, the Quaker world, the world of cancer sufferers. The poor cancer sufferers and their carers were devastated to suddenly find him gone. When I told them as gently as I could, I felt as if I was knocking a solid plank from beneath their feet. Some were deeply affected. They had believed he could make it. He had said he would and they had had faith. The cynics must have had a field day.

There is always a great deal to do after a death. I didn't realise how much letter writing and hanging on the phone I should have to do while things were sorted out. The will, the new pension arrangements, tax, finances generally. Not interesting to write or read about, but draining in the extreme.

*

I have already mentioned our interest in the ideas of Spiritualism. We had investigated over the years, read, attended lectures at the College of Psychic Studies in London, and also services at The Arthur Findlay College at Stansted Hall which is owned by the Spiritualists' National Union.

Stansted Hall, only twelve miles from the cottage, is a sort of Mecca as far as Spiritualists are concerned. Placed right on the perimeter of Stansted airport, the Victorian Gothic mansion and its adjoining long, glass-roofed chapel look out over a huge lawn, rose beds and magnificent trees. More trees and parkland with grazing animals lie beyond. The place is a hive of activity, with people travelling from near and far to attend the courses that are run there all year round. At one time we regularly attended services in the chapel (and Martin occasionally helped out as organist), and saw demonstrations by the finest mediums in the country. This made us very familiar and at ease with the process and with the different ways in which mediums work.

We both had messages ourselves at different times, and over the years took along various friends to share in the experience. I remember two occasions on which friends received messages.

The first was a message of love from her father for our friend, Shirley. The medium began by saying she was finding herself desperately searching a house for some small object which had been lost. When she went on to identify it as an RAF cap badge, Shirley immediately and excitedly confirmed that this had indeed happened. Her father had been in the RAF and she had kept his cap badge as a treasured memento. She had lost it sometime after his death and had turned the house upside-down in her efforts to find it. He had obviously been watching her.

On the second occasion there was also a connection with flying. We took a friend, whom I will call Tessa, to a service when she was in desperate grief after a tragic accident. She had recently begun a relationship with Ned (also not his real name), who had been introduced to her by his ex-wife, a friend of Tessa's at the time. A few days after their first meeting they knew they were falling in love.

Tessa writes:

About six months after we'd met, Ned asked me if I would live with him and I said 'yes'. He told me on the Friday before the accident he had found us a house and I was to look at it later the following week.

Both Tessa and Ned were at the time training to get their pilot's licences, and on the Sunday afternoon Ned went flying and was killed when the plane crashed.

I 'heard' him say 'I love you' but he never finished the 'you', it was cut off halfway through. I felt a devastating sense of loss, and burst into tears.

My friend (his ex-wife) rang a couple of hours later to tell me about the accident. The pilot flew Ned and another passenger into a thunderstorm. A wing of the light aircraft had broken off.

He still loves me and 'visits' me nearly twenty-seven years later. I know when he's around as I get the same warm internal glow that I used to get when he was present in life.

Tessa knew Ned was desperate to speak to her so, only a matter of a few weeks after his death, she came with Martin and me to a Sunday evening service at Stansted Hall. There was a congregation of about a hundred all eager to have a message but Ned came through strongly and with great urgency. The medium said his passing had been very sudden, and 'picked up' a plane crash; she also said it was very recent, and he was with his grandmother now, and that he said he was fine.

In addition to the message of love for Tessa, she was also requested to act as a messenger. Ned was asking if she would please tell his ex-wife that he was all right and give her his love. She was able to pass on the message.

Tessa writes:

I spoke to the medium afterwards and she said it was unusual for someone to come through so quickly and so strongly, after only 3 weeks.

Some years later after I had learnt to fly and got my licence (which I felt I was doing for Ned as well as myself as he had never had the chance), I went back to Stansted Hall and saw a medium called Simon James. He could quite clearly see Ned in the room with us and told me all sorts of things no-one else could have known. He mentioned 'seeing' a pink glass lady, and was very puzzled until I explained it was an ornament I still have. Ned had picked it up to admire it, not realising it was in three sections. The bottom dropped off and smashed in the hearth. He was mortified, and though I said it didn't matter, it was clearly still bothering him on the other side! He also mentioned my 'elephant' earrings. I said that didn't mean anything to me, but when I got home my son reminded me that my sister had sent me a pair of tiny 'elephant' earrings made of some kind of semi-precious stone. By the time I met Ned I'd lost one and he had commented on me wearing odd earrings and said he'd get me a matching pair!

Simon could also see Ned looping across the sky in a yellow plane: his greatest joy in life was to fly. He asked about a plane called something like 'Belle' or 'Silver Belle'. It meant nothing to me at the time but a couple of weeks later when flying with a friend of mine I realised that the name of the plane was 'Nellie Bell'! As I had forgotten this name at the time I visited Simon he had no way of knowing it except through Ned.

Simon could also 'see' ring binders and told me that Ned said I was doing the right thing in studying at this time. I continued my studies, gained my Commercial Pilots Licence, and went on to be a Flying Instructor for some years. Again I felt that I was doing it for both of us.

*

We had our first experience of visiting a medium for an individual sitting in June 1979, just three years after we were married. It was arranged for us by a friend, and was a bit of a 'baptism of fire', as the elderly lady was a direct voice medium who worked in total darkness. Direct voice mediumship has become rare these days so we were very fortunate. The medium went into a deep trance and when she woke at the end of the session her return to consciousness was an obvious struggle and she clearly had no idea what had taken place. The voices, when they came, were distinct and individual and they did not come from the mouth of the medium, but from elsewhere in the room.

I felt extremely nervous to begin with. I sat gripping Martin's hand, staring into the pitch-black and listening to the medium's breathing. After a short pause her guide took charge and with a gentle, reassuring voice gradually put us at our ease. Some of her advice and comments I will include as they are recorded on the tape, because they were very helpful.

... you will both benefit from a study, not of the occult necessarily, but of what is wrongly called the afterlife - it is not the afterlife, it is the continuity of life. You throw off your body as you throw off your winter coat. It doesn't alter you. You are the same person and you continue to remain the same even if

you come back in other guises - you, the essential you, remains the same. It is the study of these things that you should make a priority... The majority of people go through life wondering if there is something or if there isn't. They come to us frightened. They shouldn't be. It's merely opening a door, and then coming out of one life into a better proportion of life. Once you can understand all this you can do an immense amount yourself in allaying other people's fears, which I do feel is important... because it is a big step, a step of necessity into the unknown... so much you have to take on trust.

You come here (to the Earth) with the slate wiped clean. However many times you've lived before, you start again with a clean slate and you have to make your marks upon it. If you came with prior knowledge it would give you an unfair advantage so you come again, quite clear, quite empty. It depends what you do in this life what your progress will be when you come out of this life. But there must be no fear. The majority of people who die don't feel anything - it can look alarming but it is just the struggle of the person to get away from the body. It's a normal thing, as normal and natural as birth, and certainly not nearly as painful. And therefore the more you can find out, the easier it becomes and the more you can help other people.

People have a very confused idea about the afterlife. There is no heaven or hell in the accepted sense. The only hell I've known is when you come here and you're forced to realise, well, did I do all those silly things? Did I make all those silly mistakes? And there's no need of it. With knowledge, with understanding, you can avoid so many of the pitfalls and I do think this is important.

You must wait for others to give you an opening. If they ask, yes, you can say as much as you know. Everyone has free will. You mustn't impose your will on anyone, anymore than they must impose theirs on you. If they ask, you will be frank and say what you know, but you've no authority to inflict your views on other people. When they themselves are in despair, they will approach you. It's only when people are at the lowest ebb, when perhaps they've lost someone that they feel has gone for ever, then they become concerned. Reassure them that it's not for ever. It's just for a small while. And they can contact them if they so desire.

Martin's guide then presented himself. He was a formidable figure whom I found somewhat alarming. He was protective, supportive and understanding of Martin, but his demands were clear and unequivocal. Great things were expected. Martin must study and continually find new areas of life into which to delve. *"I want all things new!"* he said. When the time came for Martin to go into the next world the life he took over must be rounded and complete. Martin was told he had healing abilities and that he must prepare himself to speak at and lead meetings. But he was also told: "Life is for living… I also found time to live!"

We still had a great many family problems at the time and we were told to offer help, but not to get too involved. Not to try to pick up other people's burdens. This was a good lesson for us, and one we both took to heart.

This is something you must both guard against. I feel this for both of you. Help, give instruction, guidance where you can, but remember each of you is a world in yourself. You must not take on others' burdens. Show them the way, point them the pathway, but when you become personally involved your viewpoint becomes distorted.

My guide was gentler and spoke haltingly in English with a distinct Chinese accent. She said she had been a priestess in Peking seven hundred years ago and she would help me heal the sick in body and in mind. I have never felt I have lived up to her expectations of me, but I have never forgotten her message!

When the session was almost over I asked to speak to my father and had a short but totally convincing conversation with him. It was astounding, the high point of the whole experience! It was just as if I'd picked up a telephone and suddenly heard his voice again. One cannot mistake the voice of someone who has been so close: the tone was his, the words he chose and the emotions behind the words. He reassured us about the ease of passing from life into death, though he said he had been fearful at the time. He said he was often at the cottage and that he wanted his love passed to my mother. He was delighted that I had married Martin since his passing. Although he had not known him in life, he now thought he knew Martin *better than I did*.

For days after the session we went around on a little cloud. We felt we had received something unique and tremendously confirming of all that we believed in, and of our future path. With the fear of death removed what serious fears remain?

Over the years that followed, Martin was frequently conscious of his guide. In meditation, or when his brain was partially disengaged during an automatic task such as shaving, messages would pop into his head about new directions to take. And he did try to embrace "all things new". He studied the computer and became very proficient without any outside help. He trained as a healer. He learned Esperanto, and new worlds opened up for him as a result. Then for his work as a planning consultant, he studied the effects of factory farming on the environment – this had been his specialisation in the latter years - and finally, his great love, pottery, required hours and hours of study as he laboured away to perfect his craft. He was particularly interested in the components which formed the glazes. His notebooks were filled with chemical formulae, and strange little packages were always arriving from that centre of the pottery world, Stoke on Trent.

*

Paul Beard, in his excellent book Hidden Man, quotes from the guide, or teacher, who adopted the name 'Silver Birch'.

I am not an infallible spirit teacher who never makes mistakes and has achieved the summit of progress. That cannot be so ...because the more you achieve, the more you realise that there is more <u>to be achieved</u>...

We never ask you to take us on trust. We do not say that you must do what we suggest. Nor do we insist that there are no other ways by which you can obtain a greater attunement with the Great Spirit.

What we do affirm, and with all the strength at our command, is that the truths of the spirit can be tested by your reason, intelligence and experience. There is no threat of punishment if you say we have told you things which you do not accept...

If anything we say from our life cannot pass the bar of your reason and makes it revolt, if it insults your intelligence, reject it.

We have to appeal not to the lowest, but to the highest within you, so that you will give your co-operation and allegiance because you desire to do so.

Silver Birch, although his strength and wisdom are evident, sounds as if he is standing in the background with a gentle hand on the shoulder of his student. The other guides I have heard channelled or have read about sound the same. They too have a light touch.

However, Martin undoubtedly benefited from his association with his more dominant guide. I think that at this time in his life he needed to feel that there was a definite plan he was being encouraged to follow. He had been in turmoil at the time of his divorce and separation from his children, and in the same year, 1974, he had also lost his job in the local government reorganisation and been forced to move out of his home area in order to find work.

I think that the firm hand of his guide, as revealed at that sitting, gave him a sense of identity and purpose which was to prove invaluable. Here was a father figure who was positive about his potential and path through life, and had complete faith in his abilities. Demanding? Yes. But Martin responded well to that. He had it in him to do so, and, as his guide well knew, he loved a challenge.

*

So, you will see that though the mid-winter after Martin died felt painful and strange, it was by no means entirely bleak and without hope. I am not naturally psychic, and the odd little intimations that he was around me at times were nothing that I could prove or even totally believe in myself. There was, however, a confidence that he had not gone far, and I hoped that it was only a matter of time before I was able to be in contact with him again.

I made an appointment to visit Paul Lambillion.

Chapter 6

"I'm only a thought away"

I booked an appointment with Paul for 22nd January, 2004, just a month after Martin died, but, as I entered the study at his home in Bury St. Edmunds, I didn't know quite what to expect.

Paul is a spiritual healer and teacher and has years of experience of working with individuals and groups in many parts of the world. His gifts are remarkable and he has developed them to the point where contact with those in other dimensions is part of his everyday life.

Martin had visited Paul on two occasions. On the first they talked at some length, so Martin's character and interests were known to Paul. On the second occasion a month later, on December 18th, they had a half hour session together during which Paul gave healing. Martin died on the 21st.

Paul was in his usual good spirits and after a brief chat I felt able to ask him if he would see whether he could make contact with Martin. The communication which follows I have taken directly from a cassette recording.

"Right," he said. "I'm going to put on my other hat. I don't know if we will get the young man, but you never know! (Paul is nearly ten years younger than Martin but always refers to him as the "young man".) There was a slight pause and Paul gazed into the middle distance at a point just next to where I was sitting.

"Right!" he said suddenly, "we have two or three people who've popped through." My heart did a somersault, " - just as a matter of interest have you got a nice garden?"

"Quite nice. Yes. He was very keen on it."

"Well," Paul went on, "there's somebody here taking me into a garden and I have a feeling that it's him. And I'm just looking round. Did you have any pots or tubs in which -?"

"Well, it's his pottery!" I burst out.

I realized that Paul had seen many people since his last session with Martin and really didn't have a clear memory of their conversation. But things were beginning to come back to him.

"Well, of course! D'you know, how stupid can you get? I'm being shown all these pots outside. Has he got some of his own in the garden?"

"No," I said, "they're too big for his kiln but he's probably wanting to take you -"

Paul held up his hand, "No, don't 'lead' me. We're just taking a look around. He's showing me pots with things growing in them but, of course, that's leading us to POTS, isn't it? OK. Have you got a patio or a paved area because he was showing me that as well. I think he quite liked to be there and to ruminate and reflect - that's what we have - I can actually see him and I just want to make sure that that's right. Did he keep diaries at all? Or notes?"

"He kept a diary on his computer to do with cancer," I said, but that was obviously not what Paul meant.

"Right. No... I know what this is! It's to do with experimenting. It's surely to do with trying to... He liked experimenting, didn't he? Did he ever make glazes because this is to do with glazes, you know?"

"Yes! Yes!"

"Like, you know, you have a bit of this and a bit of that…" said Paul gesticulating and getting thoroughly involved in the process.

"Yes!"

"You bung it in and when it reaches 1000 degrees the cones melt," said Paul, recollecting his personal experience of making pottery. "There must be some notes that he's kept about glazes or something of that kind, because that's what he's talking about."

"Yes!" I said emphatically. Martin had bulging files and notebooks on a shelf beside the kiln.

"There was something he was trying to get, he's telling me, before he became really ill," Paul went on. "There was some glaze he was trying to get right. He couldn't because it was crazing or something and this is what these notes are about. They're about the glazes. The shiny bits on the outside of the pots! Oh, yes, we're getting there!"

All this I could corroborate. Martin was forever working to get his glazes exactly as he wanted them and often there were disappointments.

"What else, young man? … Right… OK. Have you got a son?"

Paul then went on to relay Martin's thoughts about Mike and how he was coping.

"Did you speak to him yesterday?"

"Yes," I said. I had had a phone conversation with Mike the evening before.

"Because he says he 'went over' to his son yesterday.

What they mean by that is they make themselves present there somehow. And he 'went over' yesterday. So it's possible that you would have had a conversation with this son about him yesterday."

I agreed that I had. Paul said Martin had been around while the conversation was going on, and that Mike was picking up from being upset about losing his Dad.

Paul's mind (and Martin's) was working fast and Paul suddenly interrupted himself to say, "You've got nothing to do with boats, have you? Not really?"

"Well, we live at a place called Saling"[1], I said.

"Oh, of course you do," said Paul. "I can see sails."

"Yes. But also when I first met him we were looking at a boat."

I then realized that Martin was remembering an agreement we had made some years ago, that 'Saling' or 'sailing' would make a good word to use as a test during a possible future communication when one of us had passed on. Paul went on to say that he was seeing a sailing boat and that Martin had used the word 'poignant', and added that it was like the beginning of a journey.

Indeed it was! Early in the process of getting to know one another in Aberystwyth we had a long conversation sitting on a seat on the seafront, watching the sun set behind a small sailing boat with red sails. I think we were too shy to look at each other so we both always remembered gazing intently at the little boat in the sunset.

"And now, what's he showing me?" Paul asked himself. "He's just handed me a watch. What are you giving me the watch for, young man? Was there some sort of unusual watch?"

---

[1] Pronounced 'sailing'.

he asked me. "When I first saw it I thought it was one of those watches you wear in the water. Because it's black."

I said that I had been looking at a watch of Martin's the evening before, when I had emptied his anorak pockets. It was a waterproof one that he used for pottery because his hands were always in water.

"Was it still going?" asked Paul.

"Yes," I said.

"Because he's saying 'it's still going.' And it's got a black strap?"

"Yes."

"That's the one. That's the one."

"Lovely!"

"Yes," said Paul. "He's obviously aware of you doing things and putting things away. It's a working watch, an everyday watch. That's often the kind of thing that has the strongest memory. And a bit of information that I've got here. 'It's a game. It's a game, you know.' I think he's talking about life and he now realizes that you do the best you can with it. The word 'game' was used, not in a derisory sense, but it's something you explore. You don't quite know how it's going to work out but you do the best you can with it. You know, trying to improve. And that's something that he was very conscious of, wasn't it? You know, trying to get things better. Trying to improve? And I've actually had the words 'I can see more clearly now. And see the game.' That's actually being said to me."

The next part of the communication concerned his mother and my mother who seemed to be with him. Paul described a scene of domesticity with knitting needles clicking and some mouth-watering traditional cookery going on. I can imagine the sceptics shaking their heads. However, such familiar sights and scenes taking place in familiar settings are very often described in communications. It seems that Earthly conditions are replicated to make the new arrivals feel at home. But equally, how are we to recognise loved ones unless we see them occupied in ways we remember? Because they are shown to us sewing, knitting, cooking or gardening this doesn't mean they don't have spiritual learning, tasks and recreation which they are also (and perhaps mainly) engaged in.

Martin returned to the theme he loved the best. Paul said he could see him quite clearly now.

"He loved his pottery, didn't he? He really did. Because he keeps going back to it all the time. And … are you going to keep the kiln for the time being?"

"Well, this is what I want to ask him."

"Because he said, 'What's she going to do with the kiln?'"

"I know. I know. I don't know whether to try and change it - the pottery - into something else."

There was more conversation about the pottery, the essence of which was that I must do what I thought best. Martin had designed the building so that it could be converted into a small dwelling, and it seemed he didn't want to impose on me the need to keep it as it was.

"Well," said Paul, "he showed me the kiln and the space round it and he said…he's …the impression I got …I'm just going back again to tap into …yes, definitely, you must do what you want to do. You mustn't do something because of him. 'Don't do it because of me. Do what *you* think is right. It would be nice if somebody could still use it but if they don't, then you'll have to rip it out. Change it. Change the building.' OK? That is nice. They usually do say that."

"Right."

"They say '*You've* got to live it now. Not me. *You've* got to do what *you* want.' But he said 'Maybe wait a little while yet before you make a decision'... Is there any connection with the month of March? An anniversary? He's lighting a candle."

We were off on a new direction. Martin seemed to know about a little break I was planning with my three nieces in March and he said it would do me good. Then Paul said he was showing him large flowers. Were they dahlias or chrysanthemums? I doubted it, as neither of us liked either. Paul was feeling a little horticulturally challenged, I think, but eventually I realised Martin must be showing him a passion flower. He had once embroidered a cushion with a design of passion flowers and he was very proud of it.

"He made the cushion?" Paul asked.

"Yes."

"Ah! Because there's this big flower and it's a sort of pinky-red. Yes. He keeps taking me back to this flower. He was proud of that. He says, 'Good with m'hands. Good with m'hands.'... Was he interested in building at all?"

"Oh, yes. He designed the pottery. He was a planner."

On and on went Paul. I found the communication totally convincing but I didn't have time to feel too emotional about this wonderful connection because the words were coming so fast. As we switch-backed from one subject to the next, I appreciated how rapidly the mind can work when not restricted by the physical nervous system.

"Well," said Paul, "he's brought you a bunch of flowers. Not just one kind. But mixed. Which is lovely. Like garden flowers. And he's also," and Paul laughed heartily, "Ha! ha! - sense of humour - he's brought you a pot! As if you haven't got enough already. A little pot! Was there one he made for you at some point?"

"Ah! Well, there were so many," I said, fondly.

"Not very big. And some flowers. He laughed at the pot and said 'As if she hasn't got enough already'. It's rather sweet, isn't it? ... And he says 'Take the break. It'll do you good. Have a break... That'll be rather nice.' I mean I can see him quite clearly standing by you with his cap on, because he wore a cap sometimes, didn't he?"

"Yes," I said.

"Yes. He's standing right next to you. There."

I smiled affectionately at what to me was a blank space.

"Have a break. That'll do you good... Did he do drawing as well? 'Cos he's taken this book out of a bag. He's got a bag. It's all diagrams or something."

There was more about the little book Martin had always carried with him in which he would sketch shapes for the pots he wanted to make. And then –

"He said you can clear out what you like now. He's showing me a big broom. 'You can clear out what you like.' He doesn't need it right now. It's a great big broom like a yard broom. 'Give it a good old tidying up. It's important things are lived in.' 'Cos he believed in life and living. 'It's important things are lived in.'... D. The initial D."

"Yes!" I said.

"Well there's a person called Dee. D.E.E. who – is there a connection?"

"Yes. She gave him some therapy."

"Yes. That's it. That's it. Because it's to do with his healing and so on. And he said, someone, Dee, who helped him."

"Yes. What does he want?"

"Just to be remembered. Yes. So 'thanks for doing my feet.' She did his feet. Reflexology or something?"

"That's right."

" 'Thanks to Dee.' I thought she was a therapist 'cos he's showing me a white coat. I know she probably doesn't wear a white coat but it's symbolic. I think she helped him quite a bit actually. And ... I can't understand that. Don't know if I'm hearing it right…the word 'stooge'?" Paul sounded puzzled.

"Stage. I'm interested in theatre."

"Oh! Oooh! He had quite a sense of humour, didn't he?"

"Yes."

"There's something here and - I've only just worked it out. D'you ever act in plays?"

"Yes."

"He said ,'You can't do this one.' And he's given you a skull. And …um…I couldn't put this together because I wondered if you were interested in cranial things? But there's no interest in anything like that, is there?"

"No," I said, racking my brains, "He gave me a pair of earrings. You know, the masks. The masks of comedy and tragedy. They're rather like skulls."

"The muses. Yes. No, no, no, … Are you in a play?"

"I'm directing one."

"No. Because this is 'Alas, poor Yorick'. The skull. From *Hamlet*."

Suddenly everything fell into place. It was thrilling! "Oh, I've got the book! On the table! I read a lot about the theatre and I've got a book on the kitchen table that's about eighty-eight different productions of *Hamlet* that someone had seen. It's by a theatre critic. And the picture on the front is of one of them holding the skull. Paul Scofield, I think. And it's on the kitchen table!"

"Yes," said Paul, "well, he's aware of that. I wondered what on earth the skull was doing. Well, it's either something you're reading or…something. He's just brought the skull through. 'Alas, poor Yorick, I knew him well.'"

We both laughed in delight at this clever little touch. I could imagine Martin on his trip round the cottage the evening before. Getting suddenly very bold, I said, "Could you ask him what he thought of his funeral?"

"What did you think of your send-off?" said Paul to the space beside me and then listened attentively. "Oh, he says it was good. It was all right. I've not got any real comeback. Why? Did you do something different?"

I must admit I was a little bit disappointed. "Yes," I said. "He had a woodland burial. It was Green. I thought he'd approve."

"Oh, yes. He said it was fine. I've got a big tick next to it…Did he like a glass of beer? He never made his own, did he? At any point?" Paul was miming holding a glass.

"He may have done. He tried most things," I said. I must admit I felt a little annoyance at this apparent flippancy.

"Was there a beer at his funeral?" asked Paul.

"Well," I said almost truculently, "we had a bit of a 'knees up' afterwards."

It was a week later that the truth dawned! Beryl, who was

reading through the transcript, suddenly said, 'Not a beer, a bier!' It certainly hadn't dawned on me. Once I'd seen Paul apparently holding a glass I'd completely lost the plot. Paul had put his own interpretation on Martin's words, unless Martin was deliberately misleading him with a double meaning.

There was a little more light-hearted chat about celebrations and then Martin changed track again.

"He says you'll do something interesting drama-wise in the autumn. I don't know what it is but it may be October time," said Paul.

"I'm hoping to go to a drama festival but I don't know when it is."

"No. This is something that you're going to do yourself. I don't know what it is. In front of you he's got a what do you call it?"

"A script?"

"Yes, that's right. And you're putting pencil marks in it like 'enter, stage right'."

"Oh. I've written a play that was *going* to be performed, but now it's fallen through."

"Well, keep your fingers crossed because something's going to be done to enable you to see this through. And for some reason October is important in relation to this play of yours. Could be interesting. He says you must keep going on that. He's giving you a pen and some blank paper, which is lovely. I always get excited about a pen and a new pad."

This proved correct. In October I joined *WriteOn*, a Cambridge group for writers and actors, which in those days put on sketches and short plays in the basement of a student café, every Sunday evening. Over the next two years or so, several pieces of my work were performed there, and being part of this lively group of creative people – mostly much younger than myself – was a great support and stimulus to me as I gradually began to find my feet again.

Back to the session, and Paul was saying, "Oh, he says 'The swelling's gone now.' That's a joke, of course. He says 'We don't have swelling over here.'"

"Oh good! ... How's the hearing? Is he enjoying hearing?"

An amazing thing happened next. Martin had had digital hearing aids but, living life the way he did, they were always in the wars. He would regularly drop them, sit on them or put them through the washing machine. So one was usually out of action. When a damaged aid had been mended and he was hearing clearly again I would say something so he could check the volume level and he would tease me by saying "Pardon?"

"Pardon?" said Paul quick as a flash, and burst out laughing. "I take no responsibility for that poor joke. He said 'say pardon?' Sorry, what was it again?"

"How's your hearing?" I repeated, laughing.

"A little voice said 'Pardon?' I don't think they have any trouble 'auditorily' over there. They pick up thoughts telepathically and they transmit back and this is basically what he's up to. Something very interesting here. He's showing me things - I thought it was freemasonry at first - he's showing me a setsquare and things like that. I mean I know they're building things but I wondered if there was anything...I'm not sure."

"Drawing?"

"Could be. Did he ever use compasses? Things like that?"

"Oh, yes. I'm using his drawing board. I've moved into his office and I'm using it as a table."

"Right. That's why he's showing me the bits and pieces connected with drawing. Absolutely. But once again he's told me that you must do what you want to do both with the building and everything else. But he'll be around. He said 'I'm not going far.' And he's used a phrase that was once put into my head some years ago. He says, 'I'm only a thought away.'"

There was a bit of banter between Martin and Paul at this point followed by another serious moment.

"Interestingly enough," reported Paul, "he says that the B17 *does* work. It *does* do something. It does improve the system. It does help. He knows that now. He didn't get to the other side thinking that it was a failure. It's important that you know that…Have you had to do a lot of washing, or washing up, or scrubbing?"

"Well, I'm cleaning his office."

"He says, 'Put your 'Marigolds' on!'"

"Well, I'm finding surfaces that haven't seen the light of day for years."

"They might need a bit of a wipe over. Because he's watched you with your 'Marigolds' on. Doing your bits and pieces. He's quite aware of what's going on. Anyway he wants you to know that he's about a lot and he's only a thought away. And he'll pop through again at some point."

There followed some talk about other family members, and wanting his love sent to his children, and then, as Paul puts it, Martin 'loosened up' and the communication was over. I said how grateful I was, and Paul said:

"Well, he was determined to pop through. I'm very pleased. You can't always be sure. Sometimes it takes months or even years before someone makes a connection. It varies enormously.

I've seen people at their own funerals watching what was going on. Equally, with a friend of mine who believed in this sort of thing, it was five years! So, there's no rhyme or reason – well there is – but not one I can understand."

Paul asked me how I was doing and said I seemed to be OK. I said I was, and added that an understanding of the afterlife and sessions such as this helped tremendously.

"Well, I hope so," said Paul. "Some people can be very condemning and say it's 'communing with Satan' and gets in the way of grieving. I don't think so. I think it helps the process. I'm infuriated by this attitude. It's based on fear and ignorance. Looked at the right way it helps to show the bigger picture and the continuity of life. All civilizations have done this kind of thing. *Why shouldn't we?*"

After some more chat the session ended, and I came out of Paul's house and blinked in the daylight. Everything was changed. I felt light and joyful. Martin had arrived on the other side and was happy and functioning well. It was a long time since I had heard him in such good spirits. He was his old self again, as he had been before the illness. I could let those last sad images go and picture him in full health.

I wished he was back with me again in that state. I could do with his strength with all that I had to do! Confusion. A huge pang of sadness for what was lost mixed with the joy of reunion. And yet his strength and support *were* with me, and in a way he felt even closer than he had in life.

"I'm only a thought away!"

*

As I stood on that pavement in Bury St. Edmunds, I was

clearly on a high. Even the tinkling refrain from a passing ice cream van seemed to have a heavenly tone to it! Time to look at what had happened with a cool head.

Although Paul has always experienced the world in his own unique way, what he describes is at first quite bewildering to the average person. And, of course, it is all open to question. Are there *really* spirit people present or does Paul have a very vivid imagination and a huge power of memory recall and invention? It is right to approach the experience with a certain amount of open-minded scepticism, as I am sure he would himself agree.

There is his reputation to consider. He has developed the gifts he was born with and used them carefully and responsibly to help others over many years. There are hundreds who would testify to the accuracy of what has been relayed to them. I have met quite a few of them myself.

I was used to the way mediums *usually* work, and this experience had been very different. Usually the sitter is requested to remain passive, and only answer 'yes' or 'no' in reply to information given. It is unusual for a medium to have met and spoken with the sitter (let alone the communicator!) before the sitting commences. The best test that communication is genuine is, of course, for the medium to relay information to a sitter who remains anonymous (or uses a false name), whom they have never met. These conditions will be strictly adhered to by most professional mediums so that they cannot be accused of gathering information which they will later re-cycle. Fraudulent mediums, if given the chance, will make every effort to discover as much as possible through casual conversation.

None of these rules apply to Paul's sessions because he is not *principally* working as a medium and does not give sittings. His ability to link a person on Earth with their loved ones in spirit is secondary to his work as a spiritual counsellor and healer. He simply relays, during the course of a healing or counselling session, communications from spirits who have made themselves known to him as being close to the human being physically present. He says they often appear to him early in the morning of the day of a person's appointment and wait around until their moment arrives.

(When I walk into Paul's study, usually at eleven o'clock, he often says: "Martin's been here since nine!")

Martin and Paul had met on two occasions and talked of all sorts of things, so Paul could be consciously recalling information or drawing on what was stored in his sub-conscious mind. Equally, Paul and I had talked at the beginning of the session. However, the most significant parts of the communication for me concerned matters that neither Martin nor I had talked about with Paul. Some concerned events which were yet to happen, some concerned small details that were only known to Martin and myself, some concerned the events of the evening before, which I had not discussed with Paul.

The references to what was happening in my life were very accurate. So, was Paul drawing on my mind telepathically? This also is a possibility. If we continue along this path of inquiry we inevitably encounter the complicated theory of Super-ESP. (Super-extra sensory perception.)

As David Fontana explains:

The Super-ESP or Super-PSI argument has it that all the information obtained through mediums could come not from the deceased but from sources on Earth. They may receive it telepathically from the mind of the sitter (even though the latter may not consciously be thinking about the information at the time), telepathically from the minds of people elsewhere, clairvoyantly from the environment, or even precognitively from the future moment when the sitter checks on the facts given in the communication and finds them to be correct....

Finally, even if the Super-ESP explanation could be shown to be true, it would by no means destroy the case for survival. In fact it could be argued that it would support it in that it would reveal that the mind has a quite extraordinary ability to operate outside time and space (which ...appears in itself to strengthen the evidence for survival, since death simply means coming to an end within the time-space continuum).

(David Fontana. *Is There an Afterlife? A Comprehensive Overview of the Evidence.*)

*

Writing now, in 2009, I have thirteen cassette tapes of (approx.) 45 minutes duration of my sessions with Paul. Not only has he seen and talked to Martin, but also Martin's mother, my parents and other members of my family. These briefer contacts come from spirit people who are having more difficulty communicating or are just happier to hover in the background. Sometimes they are just mentioned but don't even speak. Martin is pretty well always in the foreground throughout the sessions, seeming to facilitate the others. Also present, I believe, are Paul's guides and helpers, and, at times, my own.

It is usually true with mediumistic communications that the stronger personalities come to the fore, and act as a sort of master or mistress of ceremonies, sometimes enjoying the opportunity so much that the medium has difficulty in 'loosening up from them'! It is unusual for family members further back in time than the grandparent generation to communicate, perhaps because the personal link is likely to be lacking. Communicating with Earth does not seem a particularly easy thing for spirit beings to do, but those who have an aptitude for it and have mastered the technique are keen to get in touch. Love and need are the strongest motives for making contact.

Paul's contact with Martin is robust – if I can put it like that. He experiences Martin as being present in the room, speaking to him or showing him mental pictures. Sometimes, Paul says, the sound he hears is a bit distorted, not unlike short-wave radio, so he is not sure of certain consonants or vowels. In the first session he gave me 'stooge' for 'stage', and in later sessions, 'Rick' for 'Nick', and 'Joan' for 'Jean'. This is quite a common problem for mediums, which I have encountered before.

Paul receives mental pictures, but also (as he describes it) Martin will actually move about, change hats and sometimes completely change his clothing to suit the subject matter being discussed. As Martin tries to relay what he wants to say or show, there is always the possibility that Paul will fail to interpret correctly, or I will fail to understand. Usually on these occasions Martin will let Paul know that he has misinterpreted the message, and there will be a struggle between all three of us to get to the nub of what he is trying to convey. This isn't a telephone conversation, it is communication between different dimensions, so difficulties are hardly surprising. Sometimes we have to admit defeat and then Martin quickly moves on to another subject.

Finally, what happens in these sessions is consistent with what I have been hearing about, reading about and experiencing for fifty years. And I always have the feeling that what Martin chooses to communicate has been planned in a way which provides its own proof that it comes from him. There is something very subtle at work when the communications are being given. I cannot put my finger on it, but I can feel it!

However much we read about evidence, or hear other people receive it, until we have had our own contact with a loved one, at least a degree of scepticism is likely to remain. Once a contact has been established and personal information given, I cannot count the number of times I have heard someone say, with an amazed expression, that they can now believe their loved one is still alive *because the personal information received could have come in no other way.* It is no exaggeration to say that this can be a life-changing moment.

Chapter 7

"They showed me a map"

In the first few months of 2004 a strange thing would happen as I sat in the evenings, either reading, watching TV or plunged in thought. My eldest cat, Prue, the beautiful creature with the long, dark fur and green eyes, would watch a particular armchair opposite where she liked to curl up. Her look was steadfast, fixed and puzzled, almost as if she was hypnotized. If she fell asleep she would resume her wide-eyed stare immediately she woke again. If I put my hand in front of her face she would move her position slightly so she could continue staring at the same spot. This went on hour after hour, evening after evening. Occasionally the experience seemed too much for her and she would rush out of the room. It was obvious that someone I couldn't see was sitting in that chair. It had to be Martin.

I spoke to him and asked him to move to another chair so I could see if Prue's eyes would follow. Nothing happened. I couldn't ask him to go because it was lovely to think that he was there, but I found Prue's constant stare rather distracting. *I* felt drawn to watch *her*, as *she* felt drawn to watch *him!*

I went to see Paul for the second time on April 8th and began by explaining what was happening.

"Oh, he's often there," Paul said quickly. "And there's another presence too. Has your father passed over? Did Martin know your father? I think they're present in the house a lot. I think it's to help you. Talk to them. Give them a little prayer and a blessing."

I told Paul what my father had said through the direct voice medium all those years ago, about knowing Martin better than I did. I had always thought they would get on well as they had many interests in common, so I was delighted to know that they were coming together to be with me.

"It's to bring some nice energy into the house and make you feel you're not on your own," said Paul.

The session then moved off in a different direction as Paul was shown many sheets of paper with handwriting on them. He couldn't make out the language but said it was similar to Spanish.

I realised that this might be a reference to a large collection of papers I had burnt the day before. (Paul could smell the smoke.) They had belonged to an elderly Friend, Edward Osmotherly, who was a keen Esperantist and had encouraged Martin's interest in the language by presenting him with a dictionary. When he died, Edward had left all his Esperanto books and papers to Martin. The books had eventually found good homes, but the papers had remained in large boxes in a cupboard, and in my efforts to turn out the cottage I had decided that now was the time they had to go!

I mention this because it led to an interesting conversation with Paul about *not* feeling guilty when we have to get rid of other people's possessions.

"I'm being told you should continue with the removal of unnecessary clutter. Whatever you want to get rid of, that's OK," said Paul, as if this was an important announcement.

He went on to explain that after people pass on, their Earthly personality isn't as important as it once was. They can put on the personality rather like a hat and say, "Do you remember when I was Martin?" But they've actually expanded beyond that point. They realise that a pile of papers isn't really that important. They have no attachment to material things.[2]

In his experience, Paul said, they come to give us messages of love and support but never to tell us off. It's as if they have been a character in a play. They've come off the stage and are no longer playing that part. Paul said I was being given *carte blanche* to get rid of things.

I like this idea of non-attachment and expansion and will refer to it again later in connection with Martin's feelings as he passed.

"He's pulled an armchair over. He's sitting in it. Your father's standing up. He's right beside you. Martin's got a hat on," said Paul.

This reference to Martin's hat was the beginning of a theme that was to run through the sessions with Paul. I was very slow to pick up what Martin was trying to show, and I won't bore you with all the complications that took place before I finally realised that he was wearing a Flowerpot Man's hat! Some readers will remember Bill and Ben the Flowerpot Men from the children's TV programme. Martin evidently likes the idea of combining his love of gardening and his love of pottery. As a way for me to recognise him he now always shows himself in this kind of hat, and on one occasion when I was being particularly obtuse, Paul also saw the Flowerpot Man's little green jerkin.

It is perhaps surprising that there is so much visual and

---

[2] This is Paul's experience. However, I feel I must add that I have also heard of spirits, particularly female, who communicate anxiously about where a piece of jewellery or other precious items of theirs has ended up. They are sometimes not best pleased if the 'wrong' person has inherited!

verbal fun in these sessions. People who haven't had experience of a meeting of this kind might come to it still carrying their last memories of their loved one associated with illness, death, funerals and solemnity, and expect a rather sombre communication from beyond the grave. It is not like that at all in my experience. There may be moments of deep emotion, even regret at the parting that has taken place, but our loved ones in spirit come to cheer and encourage us because they now have a vision of life which is wonderfully enlarged and full of understanding and hope.

There are exceptions, of course, when people have passed tragically and are still adjusting to their new life, but there is always help and care available for them, and in time they will usually move to a happier and more accepting state of mind.

The session then moved on again. Sometimes Paul is fed so many pictures and ideas in quick succession that it can feel rather like being on a switchback!

"Are you planning to do some writing? He can channel some of his imagination to give you a little bit of a lift as you're focusing. He has good ideas," said Paul.

After some more on this theme we were back with clearing out – my main preoccupation at this time, and something I felt I had to do before I could get back to writing.

Paul was shown the letters R.T.P.I., but in the wrong order. Yes, Martin had been a member of the Royal Town Planning Institute. Paul was then shown maps being thrown away. Later in the session we were onto photographs. I was also trying to deal with a lot of these, mainly taken on his visits to Poland. I was again told to get rid of many of them. 'Don't clutter up the place with things that aren't important!' Paul stressed the importance *spiritually* of clearing space so as to get going again *creatively*. I agreed that this was what I felt I had to do.

Martin was concerned about all the pots which were still in the pottery. A lot of them, he said, were experiments and could be broken up and used for hard core. He was also wondering what I was going to do with the building and, Paul said, he was unplugging and cleaning out the kiln.

At this point I was still hoping to let the space to a potter so it could continue to be used as Martin had intended. But I was to discover that this was not practical, and eventually the kiln *was* sold and the building converted into a little house. All this was in the future but Martin seemed to foresee that it would happen.

This brings me to another point I need to mention. There are usually predictions from Martin about things which will happen for up to about six months into the future. He highlights months or periods of time which will be important for me. He's often right. Sometimes I have to check back through the tapes and my diaries to confirm this.

At this session Martin spoke about September as being the beginning of a new phase for me. It was. I had a holiday with Margaret in Cornwall and this gave me the break and the new perspective on life that I was desperately needing. Martin also mentioned hunting in connection with the autumn, and the Bill to end hunting with hounds, which had been so long coming, became law in November 2004.

Another running theme emerged during this session. Communication through Paul's mind is difficult for Martin because it is up to Paul to interpret what he sees and hears. So, the simpler the better. Martin began to use a system of box ticking ('agree strongly, agree, disagree,' that kind of thing). This was a way of telling me what he felt about ideas and plans I might talk about in the sessions.

Towards the end of the session Paul talked about there being an old connection between Martin and me. He said we have had quite a few past lives together, a sequence, and that when we met up this time it was like a meeting of old friends. I agreed that it was.

"You had to meet again this time around, so a situation was engineered whereby you could, despite all the difficulties. It was like meeting up with an old friend and catching up on some experiences that you'd had before." Paul mentioned 'soul mates' and said it was a word he hesitated to use but that there was a connection of this sort between us.

"When you're with someone that you know is central to you being *you*, the best you can be, then whether or not they're actually a soul mate doesn't matter," he said.

"Yes," I said, tearfully, "that's what I miss."

"That hasn't gone anywhere," said Paul. "That person that makes you in touch with the real *you* - you can never lose that. He can help you be that for the next few years. But it's not bad to cry. It's natural."

Being Paul, he then told me a joke to cheer me up and ended by saying that Martin was watching my efforts in the garden, and to look out for little blue flowers coming up. Forget-me-nots. "They'll be out soon," Paul said.

"Are you making changes in the garden, too?"

I said I was, and asked if Martin approved.

"He hasn't said anything," said Paul, after listening for a moment. "But he's ticked the box for 'strongly agree'".

After that session Prue stopped staring at the armchair. I think I had made it clear that I found the experience a little unnerving night after night and the message seemed to have been received!

*

Having become more used to the process by my third visit to Paul, in October 2004, I asked if Martin could tell us what he experienced when he passed over. Martin had obviously picked up my question telepathically because he seemed very ready to give Paul the answer.

"Yes," Paul said, "you'll have to let me pause occasionally. When he first got over there he said you go into a place which is the equivalent of a reception area. That's very interesting, isn't it? He found himself sitting in a room and in this room were people he knew. His own parents were there. So his parents must be over there? Does he have a brother over there?"

"No, not a brother," I said.

"Well, there was another gentleman who met him. There was his mother and his father and this other person. It was either a friend, or a brother…someone who'd gone over before. It might even have been a work colleague who'd died, that he knew quite well."

I racked my brains but couldn't be sure who this was. And I still don't know. I have an idea it was either his godfather or the man who was his boss in his first job. He had talked about both with respect. They seemed to be mentors.

"It was someone who died before him who was important to him spiritually. It was a man wearing spectacles - thin on top," Paul went on. "He met these people in this area. You get a space that you can deal with. It was like a room. As it would be on Earth, with walls and everything. He was in this room for a while and then, he said, you are literally taken through things. To understand where you are and what has gone on and what has happened. He said, 'I looked about 40 years of age when I saw myself.' He's trying to tell us …everything is done to make you feel stable because it's quite an unusual experience. He's writing something down. Pen to paper. 'In my case they showed me a map.' That's interesting!"

I laughed at the appropriateness of this because, being a planner, Martin had always felt at home in a place, once he had seen a map. Paul and I agreed *we* wouldn't want a map!

"'For different people they do it in different ways but for me it was a map.' That makes sense. 'They showed me a map of where I'd come from. Why things had been the way they were and where … it was like a diagram and that suited my mind.'"

"Oh, yes, absolutely," I said.

"Now, is there anything else we can understand?" Paul paused and listened. "There's some name like Marianne who had some meaning on the Earth for you in the past?"

I couldn't think of anyone. Paul paused again, listened.

"He met a Being, a woman whose name was Marianne or Marianna. This person was like a teacher who gathered in certain souls to teach them the next point of what they were going to do. To take them through the next phase. He is seated with all these other Beings and they're being taught, basically. Given instructions. What comes next?" Paul asked Martin, and listened again. A longish pause.

"Ah… that's interesting. He then had a choice. You're offered a choice. You're offered what is a bit like a holiday, in effect, in your astral nature. Where you can do anything you want, have anything you want." (The astral world is the part of the spiritual world closest to Earth, in which we find ourselves after death.)

"Now that ties in with other stories I've heard," Paul continued, "to do with wish-fulfilment. You can go to a wish-fulfilment life. That's a choice. He didn't do that. He didn't feel the need. *Or* they go on to a task which is part of their growth."

I wasn't at all surprised Martin had wanted to get on with things. That was typical. There was a tantalisingly long pause, while Paul was receiving the information and then he said something which took my breath away.

"You'll find this interesting. This is surprising! He says he's been given a task which is to do with the spirits of the minerals."

"Oh, gosh, yes!" I said.

This made absolute sense. Martin's degree was in geography and had included the study of geology. I told Paul how he had loved stones and rocks and fossils and had gone on field trips with his geological hammer whilst at university. Also there was his work with glazes, and the different minerals needed to make them. Everything just fell into place!

Paul went on, "It's difficult to put into words exactly what it is he's doing. But he said that if you think that all the minerals have spirits, and his job... he's close to the Earth, and he's helping the spirits of the minerals as the Earth changes in this time. Isn't that interesting?

"He said it appeals to him very much because he has such an interest in minerals. He's helping the consciousness of the planet at this time of change. That's his main job at the moment. But that isn't all he's doing. Because, he says, you can be in more than one place at a time, in effect. It's not the only thing he does but it's something we would understand. He's also involved in prayer and he's involved in the equivalent of temple construction. It's not done physically, of course, but it's creating energy spaces which are temple-like, and he finds that interesting because he was interested in planning and form. And he says that these are tasks at the moment which are part of his remit as a soul. There are other things but he can't really explain them. He can only show me symbols and I can't understand those at the moment. He thought you'd find that interesting."

I told Paul how appropriate all this was. I felt quite overwhelmed by how wonderfully everything seemed to fit into the pattern of Martin's character and interests. I knew he would be full of wonder, and deeply involved with this new phase of his life, and with this opportunity to use his gifts and add to his knowledge. But most of all, *to be of use!* Paul went on:

"He's around quite a bit and he sends you his love. He says if you're digging in the garden and you dig up a stone, don't swear at it because he's trying to do something positive with it. He showed me a bit of flint. Gosh, this is so interesting!"

Martin always tries to bring in jokes and a general lightness. I think it's so that I don't have a chance to feel sad when we have to part.

*

As a real luxury and a therapy, I had had a plan drawn up to change the flower garden and include in it a water feature and a rose bed with an arch and a seat. One of the few compensations for a return to the single state is the opportunity to be completely selfish and please yourself! Martin hadn't liked roses because of their thorns, now I was going to have them in abundance!

The plans were drawn up in the summer of 2004 and the water feature and wooden structures put in place. But I had to wait until early spring of 2005 to buy the roses. At the end of the session in October 2004 Paul looked puzzled and asked "Martin's singing 'Roses are Blooming in Picardy'. Do you know what that means?"

"Yes," I said, "I do."

Chapter 8

"OK, step through!"

In March 2005 I visited Paul again, and early in the session, he said: "'The friends have been very supportive,' Martin tells me. With a capital 'F'? I don't know... Oh, was he a Quaker, like you? He's just put a hat on like the one on the Quaker Oats packet with the white wig."

"Can you get any more?" I asked, daringly.

"No, that's all he said," said Paul. "You're getting cunning! Testing the medium!"

"It's right," I said.

After a few more minutes of Paul not getting it, I explained that the Testimony to the Grace of God in Martin's life had recently been read in Thaxted Monthly Meeting. It had been warmly received and was being sent on to Essex and Suffolk General Meeting.

"Yes, that's it," said Paul. "I was seeing you in a meeting. He's taken his hat off."

(I have only just realised that when Martin takes his hat off - whichever hat he happens to be wearing at the time - it means that the interpretation of what he is trying to get across is correct.)

"It's probably helped him," said Paul. "Sent a nice vibe,

like prayers and things. It sends a nice light." A pause, while he checked again with Martin, and then he confirmed, "Yes, that's the gist of it."

*

I had been having dreams. They weren't particularly happy ones. I was searching for Martin, could hear his voice, knew he was somewhere in the vicinity, but couldn't actually reach him.

The settings for these dreams were never small, intimate spaces: they were large establishments which felt like colleges. In one there were people with clipboards hurrying about in a crowded hall.

Once Martin was speaking to someone outside a building – I could distinctly hear his voice – and I was on an upper floor in what was obviously his room with his possessions dotted about. It was a small study bedroom, such as might be found at a conference centre. Martin loved conferences. He had set out his possessions, made himself at home, and was now outside having an interesting chat with someone he'd met. It was such a familiar scene. I woke before I could get to him. So near and yet so far.

Once he was on the steps of a large building and I was leaving him. Once he was standing under some rather dank and dripping trees. I would wake up feeling sad.

However, I did have one very vivid dream which has stayed with me and was rather different. It came not long after he died, and I felt was to show me what his new body was like and what he could do.

In the dream, I was on the sofa in our sitting room and Martin came in and sat beside me. I was aware that I was dreaming, that he had died, and that he and I were in different dimensions.

I felt I was being given something very precious, and I sat quietly, not daring to touch him, fearful that he might be intangible or might vanish. After a moment he got up and sat down on the rug in front of the electric fire which was glowing brightly. He smiled at me, and gradually lent back into the fire, at the same time raising his arm behind his head at a completely unnatural angle. He disappeared into the fire. "Look what I can do!" That was what he seemed to be saying.

At the session in March 2005 I was describing the sad dreams to Paul, and he was talking to Martin about them. I wondered if Martin was unhappy and was perhaps going over the details of his life on Earth and feeling some regrets.

"Parting is such sweet sorrow," said Paul, which he seemed to be hearing from Martin.

"It's just the sadness at the parting you're picking up. When you're with him, you fly. It's very 'Peter Pannish'. You're in that part of the astral where you can create like an artist. 'You fly through the realms of possibility,' that's what he's saying. When you come back it's like sinking, falling. That's what you may be picking up." I was familiar with the idea that we travel in the astral realms while in the sleep state, and this sounded wonderful. I had no memory of it though.

But Paul had returned to the question of whether Martin's review of his life was causing him unhappiness, and was listening again. After a pause, he said: "Martin's not unhappy. There are always regrets, but he's worked through most of that now. He's doing things which are highly creative and which he sees meaning in."

Paul told me of the near-death experience he had had as a young man, and said: "I felt such a sense of peace and love. It was like nothing on this Earth. The only pain I experienced was the pain of coming back into the body."

"Next time you go to bed," Paul said, "think to yourself, 'I'll remember.' Because you've done loads of travelling with him and you'll do more. And you meet people you *know*. Not relatives from this lifetime, but people that you know with a capital K."

I recalled a recent incident when I had been on a train, travelling slowly along a steep embankment. The tops of the trees were below the level of the windows and I could look down into the swaying branches as we seemed to glide gently over them. I had had the spontaneous thought – this is what it's like when you fly in the astral! It was a beautiful experience.

*

Paul was aware of a father figure. He wasn't sure if it was my father or Martin's.

Then he heard the strains of Gilbert and Sullivan's *HMS Pinafore*. He began to sing a ditty which ended up 'and now I am the ruler of the Queen's Nay-vee!'

I confirmed that Martin's father had once produced *HMS Pinafore* at a school where he was a music teacher. I had seen photographs of the performance.

This was also a reference to the fact that he had been in the Navy in the Second World War, but because he was colour-blind had never been to sea. This was a clever link with Sir Joseph Porter in the operetta who, though he was 'the ruler of the Queen's Nay-vee', never actually went to sea.

"That's the joke that's going through this," Paul confirmed.

*

Although this actually happened at a later session with Paul, I will include here a contact with my own father, the most consistent communicator in my immediate family.

From the times of my earliest memories until I was in my twenties, my father, a farmer, was on the committee of the Essex Agricultural Society.

My father was always so busy, particularly during the Second World War, that at times he seemed a rather remote figure. He was acutely conscious of the huge loss of men in his generation in the First World War, and this drove him to do as much as he possibly could in public life and may have contributed to his death at only seventy-three.

In the years following World War II, I remember that the Society used to hold its annual two-day show in June, at different sites in the county. This, of course, depended on finding a landowner willing to lend a suitable piece of ground, and was not really satisfactory.

In the 1950s my father must have been on a sub-committee concerned with finding a suitable permanent site. Not only did he do a great deal of driving around Essex, but there would be endless meetings of earnest men in our dining room, puffing on pipes and poring over maps and plans, whilst they consumed large quantities of tea, coffee and biscuits provided by my mother. I can remember her rushing in to open the windows as the cars finally left, so that she could clear the fug and serve a long delayed meal!

Much to my father's relief a suitable site was eventually found near Chelmsford, and after long negotiations it was purchased. The earnest men continued to meet (puff, pore and consume) in our dining room as the new showground was prepared and the necessary infrastructure planned.

The Show was held there successfully for many years but recently it has ceased for various reasons, including the restrictions on the movement of animals due to precautions against disease, and the site has been sold. In the spring of 2008 I was driving past the site one day and saw a huge stadium with enormous lights, and many other large, ugly structures grouped around it. I hadn't driven that way for several months and had become out of touch with what was happening there, but remembered that I had heard it was to become a horse-racing track. I thought of the work my father and his colleagues had done and was saddened. There was a small group of Animal Rights Campaigners standing outside the entrance with placards and I felt I should be with them. Why hadn't I protested against the planning application?

During a session I had with Paul in June of that year, he asked, "Whose are the maps?" and described Martin and my father looking at a map or plan pinned up on a wall.

"Did your father ever campaign to save something? A meadow? Or did he have a battle over a piece of land?"

I couldn't recall anything that related to this, at first.

"It looks like a fen, or a field. It has some connection with your father…"

I then dimly remembered that some people had questioned the suitability of the proposed showground site because part of it needed draining. My father had felt that the drainage work was quite feasible and that this extra cost should not prevent the purchase of an otherwise ideal piece of land in a good location. Evidently, he and his supporters had prevailed.

"It's not the Essex Showground, is it?" I said.

"It *could* be. This place has now been changed and he's telling me he's not very happy about it. He says, 'It's been spoiled'. Is that the one at Great Leighs?"

Paul said his wife had driven past it recently and told him how awful it looked with all the floodlights.

"Your father doesn't think it's a very nice idea," said Paul. "There's a piece of land that was lovely and now it's all ... OK, it's for recreation, but it's ruined as far as he can see. He was looking at that with Martin."

Since then the company which owns the site has gone bankrupt so I don't know what use it will have in the future, but for me that was a very significant contact with my father.

He also came through a medium at Stansted Hall many years ago. The medium described him accurately and then, sounding somewhat puzzled at the message, said that he had a high IQ. As so often with me, the penny doesn't drop until hours afterwards. When my father was born there were already three Joseph Smiths alive in the family, his father, his grandfather and his great-grandfather. To avoid confusion his father was always known as Tertius, and my father, yet another Joseph, was known as Quartus, or Q for short.

*

In May 2005 I visited Brenda Hanley, a very experienced and well respected medium. I had met her once before, briefly, but she knew no details of my personal life and certainly not that my husband had died. She had never met Martin.

As the sitting began she had a very intense experience of a man with deafness, and not only deafness but tinnitus (which Martin also had), and she tuned into the acute frustration of not being able to communicate. She described how he would sometimes follow conversations by lip reading but not be able to fully take part. Another physical sensation she had was of a constricted throat. She said this usually meant disease in that area but to me it was a strong indication of Martin's stammer. I haven't mentioned this before because when he was older, and when he was with me, it was hardly noticeable, but in his early life it had been so pronounced that he had needed help from a speech therapist. It did not affect him when he was reading aloud or singing – he had been a chorister at Winchester College Choir School.

As a person with a natural desire to communicate his ideas, and who had indeed struggled to do so, he had, by the end of his life, the double handicap of a stammer *and* deafness. No wonder he was frustrated and sometimes short-tempered. He never grumbled, he would just snap.

Martin's communication through Brenda had all the familiar elements. She sensed his interest in things philosophical, his love of the natural world and his garden, and she was able to convey a great deal of emotional warmth from him to me. She had the impression of a strong personality and great intelligence. "A good communicator", she said.

When Martin and Paul are together the conversation is more on the mental level and there is a lot of humour. Martin with Brenda was quieter and more reflective. Just as we behave differently according to the company we're in, so communicators show a slightly different side to their personalities according to the medium they are working through.

Not surprisingly Martin was soon leading Brenda out into a cottage garden and towards what she described as a shed. She went with him inside the shed and found it "not very tidy!" There were books and papers everywhere…and tools. She began to focus on the tools and said he was working with wood. I said quietly, "No, not wood" (though he did sometimes do a bit of DIY woodwork) and at that point she suddenly started to be aware of the clay. She had the strong sensation of throwing a pot on the wheel and enjoying the feel of the water and clay between her hands. She said he did a bit of modelling as well but was mostly interested in throwing and making simple shapes without a great deal of decoration. True. She said he liked to be known as 'the potter'.

Martin told her that sometimes I would 'blow my top' but that I was the powerhouse of the home and a good wife to him. There was a lot of love and gratitude coming my way for having kept things going so he could concentrate on his interests. As he constantly does with Paul, Martin kept telling me to get rid of his possessions and live my own life. I find this very good advice. It helps me not to dwell in the past or indulge in shrine building. At the same time he said he would stay very close and would help me. *In getting rid of his things I would not be losing him!* Brenda and I agreed, somewhat ruefully, that the effort involved in shifting things on the Earth plane was not always appreciated by those living at higher vibrational rates where thought is action!

Towards the end of the communication Brenda said he was sitting by the pond in our garden and watching the fish. He loved to do this, especially with an afternoon pot of tea. He told Brenda he got his ideas and inspiration in this way. As a gentle farewell he wandered out of the garden and off into the countryside saying he would not be gone long. He loved to walk and be in the peace of the natural world and have a chance to reflect. All this Brenda spoke of with much feeling.

There was more of a personal nature but this was the gist of the communication, and for me it complemented the sessions with Paul as it allowed the softer side of Martin's nature to come through.

I was very grateful to Brenda for this lovely contact. She was also aware that my parents were in the background as loving presences.

*

In August '05 I visited Paul again, intent on asking Martin if he now understood *why* he had passed over when he did?

I asked this because when Martin died, at 63, he was having one of the happiest and most creative periods of his life. After only four years working as a potter, he was diagnosed with cancer. It seemed very hard.

"It's an interesting question," Paul said. "I'll see what he says. Many people pass through in a similar way when they still seem to have quite a lot to put in, good work to do on Earth. *We could do with them here!* Why, when they still have so much of a contribution do they go? I had a doctor friend who passed last year. His wife is a doctor too and she and I are both very puzzled as to why it should have happened when it did. He was a doctor who had gone into natural ways of treating people, and was very valuable. But the only conclusion I come to is that there is a greater plan and it operates in all dimensions. We have to recognise that sometimes a person is removed from here so they can work somewhere else. It's not that they aren't active. They're *very* active. But maybe being out of the body allows them to supersede what they would be able to achieve here."

Paul addressed Martin. "What have you got to say about that, young fellow?"

There was quite a long pause while he listened to the answer.

"The message I'm getting begins like this. He says he *knew* as soon as he died that he *had to go when he did*. As soon as he got through and realised he was no longer physically alive in this dimension, *he knew, he understood*, that it had to be the way it was. It was an immediate realisation. He had to move through when he did. Now I'm trying to go with what he's saying here. He said some of it was for you and some of it was for him. The reason? Let me see if I can get any more."

Strangely, as I listen to Paul, I often seem to get increased understanding myself. Not something dependent on the actual words I'm hearing but a feeling that my own vision is being slightly enlarged and lifted out of the everyday. Death is not the end: it is part of a process.

Another long pause. Then – "Interesting, it's almost as if -" Paul broke off. "In his Earth life he was a town planner?"

"Yes."

"Now he's not saying he wasn't good at it, and he didn't enjoy it, but – and please correct me if you think I've misinterpreted this – it was as if he'd at last got to the stage where he felt he could do something *beautiful*. He could do something that was not hemmed in."

"When he was doing his pottery?" I asked.

"Yes. He felt he was in a very creative phase of his life where he felt he wasn't operating with any boundaries except those he set himself. Do you understand?"

"Yes, absolutely," I said. I used to think when I watched Martin totally absorbed in throwing a pot that he was possibly as happy as any human could be. Paul went on -

"He'd reached this point and felt he was going to have some very creative years in this way. But what he's now realised is that by doing the 'boxed in' life, the disciplined, structured life that he had to do, that it freed him up to be creative."

Paul made a squeezing motion with his hands. "If you put something in a tube and then squeeze it, it comes out with more force than if it hadn't been in the tube in the first place. It's *releasing creativity*. What it did for him was that by the time he passed through, his mind was potentially in *an increasingly creative state* and he could then be creative on this higher level. Do you understand what I mean?"

I understood very well. I explained to Paul that Martin had felt more and more frustrated by his planning work, the bureaucracy he constantly faced, and the difficulties his deafness caused. His release into the visual and tactile world of pottery was a complete joy to him.

"He said that, in spite of what we think we believe, we still see this life as a complete experience that has an end to it. But he's saying that that isn't how it is at all. Death is a development in consciousness. He can *now* be very creative using both the bit of his mind that was the scientist and the logical person, with the bit of his mind that was emerging creatively, in the bigger picture. By stepping through he is able to be an *enlarged* being who can impact on things in an *enlarged* way. So, lovely as it was to do the things that he was doing here, and had just got started with, the process, the development, required him to be in this other space."

"While you're speaking," I said, "I can see that he might possibly have gone on doing much the same things as he was already doing if he had lived another twenty years."

"Quite possibly," Paul agreed. "He wanted to do something beautiful and life said OK, step through! This is the chance."

Paul paused. "I just want to tune in again for a moment, make quite sure I know what he's saying." A pause, then he continued:

"Yes. While we're here it depends on our karma, our destiny, as to which side of the veil we can best function. He's showing me a curtain and saying 'It *really is* only a curtain. It seems a big curtain when we can't see through it, but it is only a curtain and we have to make a decision as to which side of the curtain we function.' The decision is made at a higher level of ourselves. We can even fight it."

"Which he was doing," I said.

"Yes," Paul said, "because he wanted to stay here with you."

"Me," I thought, "the cottage, the cats, the pottery. The whole package was pretty good."

"That's not a good enough reason," Paul said, seeming to read my thoughts. "We *have* to go. He said he *had* to step through into this enlarged sense of self he can now function in. He's giving me this sense of *enlargement* and he says that one day *you* will have this sense of enlargement. But for karmic reasons you're meant to carry on here a bit longer than he did. You have an opportunity to be creative still in this part of the game."

Martin had talked about life as a 'game' before, of course.

"He's showing me all the crystals and minerals again. He can now see how his Earth life gave him a kind of background which would stay in his mind after death so he could still function in relation to it but with a much bigger vision. So he's not just looking at minerals and crystals but he's looking *at the planet* and its current evolution. He says it's *enthralling*. And that's what he's doing right now."

Earlier on in the session Martin had talked about the planetary changes to come.

"He says there's an enormous shake-up coming on the planet itself, in the actual geophysical nature of the planet. What we're seeing now is just the tip of the iceberg in terms of some of the transitions and transformations which are taking place; in the geophysical nature as well as the atmosphere. He's very aware of that. He's involved in the overseeing of some of the spiritual aspects of this. The impact of these changes is enormous. There is a global change. In the long term it is for the benefit of everyone. In the short term it might be a little bit tricky.

"They might discover some substances that haven't been seen before. New minerals that we didn't know existed before, coming from the heat (or the word might have been 'heart') of the planet."

Paul repeated how instantaneous Martin's realisation about the rightness of his passing had been. How *immediately* he understood. Paul likened this to the feeling he had had when he had been struck by lightning and had had an out-of-body experience.

"You look down," Paul said, "and actually you think to yourself that it's all right."

"You ask yourself do I want to go back?" I suggested. I had gleaned from my study of the subject and from talking to people who have had NDEs, that usually the experience is so wonderful that there is a reluctance to return to the Earth life.

"Oh, well, all right if I have to," Paul said, laughing. "And this is what he's saying. They get this brief moment of loss when they realise they miss the people they've left behind but that soon passes when they realise they're involved in this bigger picture. And also that this cut off from loved ones is a very temporary and slightly illusory thing anyway. It's not the same for everyone. It takes some people a lot longer to work out what's going on but he was a clever man, he could deal with these things. You'll get the chance as well. It comes to us all."

*

This is perhaps a good point to return to the predictions which are often given in a communication and which can be puzzling, especially when, with hindsight, they don't seem to have come true.

In a later session, Paul tried to explain. "The guides say that timing is notoriously difficult. They have a broader view than we do but they don't know everything. They say 'from what we can see in the next five to ten years there's a very strong chance that this or that might be revealed.' The interpretation of the message by people like me (i.e. mediums) is also a problem.

"I've made predictions or suggestions that didn't happen *when* I said they would, but when they *did* happen they happened exactly as I said they would. You get deflections in time – like a ball hitting against a wall."

Paul said that a long time ago when talking about visitors from other planets, his guides told him: "Of course it's going on. It's been going on for years but possibly by 2000 or shortly afterwards those in authority might actually say, 'We've been visited many times'."

Paul is convinced that there is more known by those in authority than we are aware of. Discoveries are being hushed up because of pressure from commercial interests.

If a cure for cancer is discovered in the next five years, would we be given access to that knowledge?

*

In any book about spiritual communication it has to be said that there is never one hundred per cent accuracy in the information given, even through a good medium. One notable and much quoted example is that White Eagle, Grace Cooke's guide, predicted that the Second World War would not happen. That was how it looked to him at the time.

Over the years I have met many people who, knowing my interest in the subject, have seized on one or two high profile examples of inaccuracies and have denounced Spiritualism, the communications, and the whole wide range of phenomena which have ever manifested on Earth, as complete bunkum. I have learned to recognize them now. They speak with a particular vehemence and a passion and a glint in the eye! They are accusing me - if not in actual words then the implication is there - of being unscientific, irrational and dangerously gullible. They are *so* strong in their denunciation that argument is completely useless. Very often I have not even said *anything,* they just know by repute that I am one of the deluded ones and need putting in my place.

All I can say is that I'm open to reasonable discussion, but when people have this kind of mindset it is better to just leave the whole thing. These are the out-and-out sceptics. They have a hidden agenda of some sort. They are looking for nothing but flaws and, when they find what they think they are looking for, it's a case of babies and bathwater!

Even if the communications were only fifty per cent accurate, and I think the figure is far higher than that, they would be worth investigation. Those who think they are the most scientific have often completely closed their minds to a proper examination of the evidence. Such encounters are painful, but I'm afraid that we have to learn to expect them and deal with them as best we can.

*

Back to 2005! During the summer I had lost my engagement ring, which is silver with a beautiful blue lace agate stone. It means a great deal to me and I was very upset, and hunted high and low. I never take it off during the day-time except to make pastry, after which I always put it straight back on again. It had to be somewhere in the cottage.

In October the kiln went back to the firm which had sold it to us. Paul had always said he had seen Martin unplugging it, and I had eventually given up the idea of being able to let the building as a pottery with living accommodation. After various setbacks I had at last obtained planning permission to turn it into a one-bedroomed house.

On a dreary day with the leaves falling and the rain pouring down, two men arrived to dismantle and remove it, telling me it would take them quite a while. The kiln had great significance for me. It was the heart of the little building and had been so magical for us both. Feeling miserable I decided to do some cleaning while I waited to give the men a hot drink when they'd finished the job.

I went to get a long-handled dustpan from the corner of the utility room, and heard something tinkle on the brick floor. Behind it was my ring. How it had got there I can't imagine. I'm not saying there was anything paranormal about it, but it was certainly returned to me on a very important day, and the message seemed to be that the kiln might be leaving but Martin was still around. It was wonderful to have it back.

"You can get rid of my pots but you can't get rid of me!"

Chapter 9

New life at the pottery

Changing the pottery into a little dwelling under its new name of 'Martin's', was a daunting task.

First I had to get it cleared. It was *full* of stuff, much of it unrecognizable to me! A potter friend came and took away buckets and small plastic dustbins full of glaze, sloshing dangerously in the back of her car. Then I contacted some professional potters through the internet. They were a married couple, both over six feet tall, such *nice* people and so *strong!* They looked everything over carefully, knew what it all was, and came back in a van to take loads of it away. They were delighted, and so was I.

Central heating had to be installed. Then the big double-garage doors had to be replaced by a front door and windows, and a kitchen fitted, and carpets laid. In the middle of all this a miracle happened. Tanya, daughter of my friends, Claudie and Tim, was expecting a baby at the beginning of December 2005, and she and her partner had nowhere to live. They were prepared to put up with anything for the sake of having a roof over their heads. (It kept reminding me of the Christmas story!)

So Tanya, Steff, Claudie and Tim, set out to help me finish sorting, clearing and cleaning the rest of the pottery in record time. The couple moved in at the beginning of November with only one habitable room – the bedroom - and their home gradually took shape around them. Steff just happened to be a professional decorator and so, in lieu of rent, he steadily worked his way through the building in any free time that he had.

Baby Torrin arrived at the beginning of December. There were initial difficulties, but he was a strong little boy, determined to live. A combination of medical science and the healing prayers of family and friends saw him through, and by the spring I was looking across from the cottage to see a happy family scene framed in the big patio-window of the little building. What a transformation!

When I went to see Paul in May 2006, Martin seemed pleased too, and remarked that the pottery was now "much more comfortable".

But first of all he showed Paul a little tree in the garden with a stake beside it. I had had a tree planted recently and it was now beginning its new life right opposite the front door of the cottage, staked for support.

"He visits often and he's pleased with what you've done with the pottery. Nothing like a clean sweep! He says it's much more comfortable now and the kiln has gone to someone who can use it. He likes to think that it's going to be used again."

Paul looked at me for confirmation of all this and I explained. And as I write this I realise there was a double meaning in the reference to 'the clean sweep'. I had had a great deal of difficulty in getting the chimney of a wood-burning stove, that Martin had used to heat the pottery, cleaned and sealed. Every time it rained a terrible smell came from it and I had had to get expert advice. This episode happened *just before* Torrin, a baby with a delicate chest, was due to be discharged from hospital. You can imagine the panic that ensued to get the job done in time, so that there were no unhealthy fumes for him to breathe!

"Oh, he's singing 'Ticket to ride'! Any connection to Eastbourne or Sussex?"

"I've just been to Poole."

"He followed you around on your travels. He didn't have a copy of *Gulliver's Travels* by Swift, did he? Did you go to a place where there was a model village with little figures?"

"No."

"All I can say is, I think this is Wimborne in Dorset."

This reminded me of a holiday Martin and I had once had in the same area when we had gone to see the model town at Wimborne. Martin had lived in Wimborne as a boy and in later life had spent a long period as a planning officer based in Yeovil. That area of the south coast was very familiar to him.

Martin's son Mike and his family live in Yeovil, and I had just returned from spending a short time with them. We had visited Brownsea Island and spent an afternoon exploring it. I explained that the singing of 'Ticket to ride' was probably a reference to the ferry boat which took us across.

That got a thumbs up from Martin.

"He's been following you around and he's very proud of the way you managed the journey. He's pleased you met up with his son."

There followed some chat about family matters which showed again that Martin was very aware of current happenings.

Later in the session, Martin was anxious to show Paul the crystals he was working with. The sight was obviously overwhelming. Paul went into a little reverie as he watched, and at times became almost lost for words.

"He's showing me these beautiful crystals again. They're

quite ...stunning...absolutely stunning. (A pause.) He's showing me...I can't even describe it...it's more fine than jewels. These wonderful minerals and crystals which come out of the Earth. He says the Earth is like a factory. People don't realise. It's continually creating anew from its core. This is why we discover new elements, because they do actually rise to the surface. It will give us all we need if we connect with it in the right way. We haven't fully understood how the Earth works. I find it fascinating... magical, sparkling, transparent."

Paul suddenly looked at me. "The car needs a service."

"Er - yes, it's going for one," I said, trying to switch my mind back to domestic matters. I certainly had to stay on my toes when Martin was around!

Later in the session Paul said: "Martin's giving your back a massage."

On my return home I had found the garden parched, and had been struggling around my favourite plants and the new tree with cans of water. My back was aching.

"He says you may wake up in the night and find your back is being worked on by little invisible fingers," Paul said.

Later still in the session Paul reminded me to ask if I need something.

"We forget to ask for what we need," he said, "but it's a most important spiritual rule."

*

"Have you done this talk you've got to do?" Paul said, five months later, during a session in October 2006.

"I have. What did he think?"

"He thought it was fine. He's giving it a tick. A bit like a teacher in a book. Where did you give it? Was it a conference, or something?"

I explained that it was a talk I'd given a couple of weeks before to Essex and Suffolk General Meeting. I had mentioned it to Paul at the previous session. I was one of a panel of four. The theme was 'Active Quakers and Quaker Activists'. The arrangements committee had wanted to hear from someone who, as far as possible, had gone through a major illness without using orthodox medical treatment, because of an ethical objection to animal experimentation. I had volunteered to speak on Martin's behalf because there didn't seem to be anyone else to do it. I told Paul it had seemed to go quite well.

Martin apparently agreed. Another couple of ticks were given.

"Yes, he says it went well," said Paul. "He was keen that you should do it. I've got a feeling he may even have prompted you to do it because of the issues. He still sees the way we treat the natural world as unethical and ...what..? what?" Paul paused to listen, then, "Yes, the way we deal with the world generally is in a very unconscious kind of a way. We don't deal with it consciously. We don't engage with it and really look at what we're doing."

Paul went on to speak about a TV programme in which someone had said "We can't experiment on people, so we use mice". Paul had wondered why.

"Just because you can't do *this*, it doesn't follow that you have to do *that*", he said, and went on, "Martin's very concerned about the Earth and its mineral resources. It's a very big thing for him at the moment. He says we're not in touch with the spirit of the planet. It has everything we need, which it can give to us easily if only we can get that consciousness right. The same is true with animals and plants and trees. We've just got to wake up. And he's pleased that you were able to present something that's linked with his thinking ... have I got that right..? Yes, he says, more or less.

"I'm interpreting what he's saying a bit," Paul explained, "because it comes to me in a strange flow sometimes. You just have to trust what you're getting. It's as if he believes that there's a lot more to be discussed on this. He also said that one day animal testing would stop. Mainly because it will be the end of pharmaceutical drugs."

*

During a later session with Paul, Martin returned to the relationship between humans and the natural world, a subject which troubles him. Paul found it a complicated message to receive and relay accurately. I will attempt a summary:

We have to turn to the mineral kingdom for our power. In the past mankind has understood the spirit of the minerals, but we don't anymore. There are changes going on in that realm, at that level. We have to turn to the mineral kingdom for the way forward in terms of power, meaning energy. In understanding matter, and particularly how matter operates through the elements, we will find out how we can have all the power we need. It's to do with the minerals and elements and particularly those which are very high in the periodic table. There will be more elements discovered. Maybe the Earth is going to throw up some more. There is a link to lasers and light technology. Martin showed Paul a town and also a penny, implying that for virtually nothing we could generate the power to provide all the energy needs of that town without damaging the planet.

*

Back to 2006! As usual Martin had been in the garden. He

was aware that the flower beds were being reshaped to make things easier to manage, and had seen the wooden lattice partition that now divided the cottage garden from the garden of 'Martin's'.

" 'Make sure you leave enough room for the flowers.' You don't need his approval but he approves of everything you're doing."

Martin also talked about the leaves in the garden which would need sweeping up, and about mushrooms which he'd loved to search for at this time of year, carrying his special basket.

"He said he used to go and pick them. Make sure you eat the right ones. Don't go on a magic mushroom trip!" This was a very typical Martin remark; he was fascinated by fungi.

"Now, he's showing me some slats of wood leaning up against a garage. I'm wondering if it's for shelves or to build something?" said Paul.

I couldn't make that out at first, and then I remembered that the roof of a covered area attached to the garden shed was rotten and needed renewing. It was leaking badly.

"He says 'not good, not good,'" said Paul. "He's got some fresh wood and some felt for the top. Oh, and the car needs checking."

*

Tanya, Steff and Torrin had spent nearly a year in 'Martin's', and were due to start a new life in France in the short winter days at the end of December 2006. Martin was well aware of the fact and conveyed his thought with a mixture of fancy dress, symbolism and a burst of music. It took a considerable time for Paul and me to unravel it all: though it was simple really, with hindsight!

Paul said he was seeing an empty basket, and hearing the *Marseillaise*. Martin had also appeared dressed as Napoleon, and waving the tricolour.

Was I taking down a hanging basket, Paul asked, between humming bursts of the French national anthem?

No, I wasn't. I had enough to do without dealing with hanging baskets!

It wasn't a real basket we realised at last, but a way of showing that once more his favourite little building was going to be empty.

*

And so we reach the end of 2006 and the end of my account of Martin's communications through Paul, which continue, of course, each time I visit him.

What do these contacts with Martin mean to me? They have helped me to understand a little about where he is now and what he's doing, and because I feel that he's happy and fulfilled I have gradually learned to let go and be happy for him. To know that he still cares and remains interested in all that I am doing, gives me great strength and a sense of continuity.

For now, I feel, our lives are running in parallel: we are each gaining different experiences and doing different work. The soul link remains. We recognized it in this life and Martin's departure from his physical body has changed nothing. I believe that at this level we spend time together when I'm asleep and perhaps at other times and in other ways that I cannot understand. I am not aware of this as yet, but it is what I have read about and been told, and I take it on trust.

Knowing these things and having confidence in them, and in the future, has given me the freedom to use the remaining years of my life on Earth as positively as I can. Life is a gift.

Since Martin's passing in 2003, as I have tried to sort out my feelings and my new path, I have been immeasurably helped by my talks with Paul. The sessions are essentially spiritual counselling, with Martin looking on and giving friendly advice. Amongst many other things, Paul has explained why I have suffered all my life from a lack of energy, and has shown me ways to try and improve this; he has also helped me to appreciate the gifts I have and encouraged me to use them. He has given me healing when I needed it. He is very wise, and his help has been invaluable: I am very fortunate to have met him.

*

I have asked my Quaker friends Sylvia Izzard and Eileen Farrah-Jones to write accounts of their own stories of contact with their husbands who have passed on, and I have drawn on these in the chapter which follows. I am very grateful to them for their contributions and hope that they will add to your understanding of this phenomenon of communication.

Chapter 10

Sylvia and Jim: Eileen and Ernie

Sylvia writes:

When Jim and I married in 1998 at the ages of 71 and 60 respectively, it was a meeting of two hearts and minds. We had both endured long, unhappy marriages previously, never believing we would find the love we both craved.

Jim had an English mother and a Canadian father, and was born in Southend-on-Sea. His father, a carpenter, helped to build the last part of Southend's famous pier. My mother was English and my father half-Scottish. I was born in Plymouth. So Jim and I, not surprisingly, both have the sea in our blood!

After spending a number of years trying to 'make it' as an entertainer/actor, Jim began what was to become a successful career in the water industry. For my part, I was a lecturer in Special Educational Needs. Jim and I were both Quakers and we met for the first time at my uncle's funeral in 1988. My aunt and uncle were also Quakers and Jim happened to be the Friend responsible for funerals at their Meeting. Ten years after that occasion we were married.

Jim had a great sense of humour and loved to make people laugh. He was also deeply spiritual. Our shared faith in God, our love of animals and all God's creation, and our appreciation of classical music, coupled with the deep bond between us, formed the foundation of our married life.

We also strongly shared a more unusual interest – the penal system. Jim had once served as a Quaker prison minister and I had served as a magistrate; as part of my training for this I had visited many prisons. Jim, for his part, had played a significant role in the release of two high-profile prisoners.

After our marriage we continued this shared interest by doing voluntary work for the Prison Fellowship - an interdenominational, international organisation aiming at restorative justice, and I have continued with this since Jim's passing.

Only six months after we married, Jim was diagnosed with Parkinson's Disease and gradually complications began to manifest. Thankfully, we had a few years when he was able to lead a relatively normal life, and the fact that we both strongly believed in an afterlife, together with our positive outlook and Jim's acceptance of the disease, meant we enjoyed nine very precious years of married life. Our deep love upheld us until, after traumatic suffering very bravely borne, Jim passed on in December 2007.

Eileen writes:

My husband Ernest, my dear Ernie, passed to spirit on Tuesday, 5th September 2000, at 4.55 am. Apart from asthma, which he developed after the death of his mother, and controlled with homeopathic remedies, he had been a very fit, active man and had planned to continue working part-time after his retirement so that we would have a little more money and could enjoy simple pursuits like cycling, walking and trips to various well loved destinations.

Unfortunately, their plans did not work out that way as Ernie developed prostate cancer from which he eventually died just twenty years after they had first met. Eileen describes their meeting in 1980 at a time when she was working as a cook-housekeeper.

I had a week off once a year and had chosen a narrow boat holiday on the Oxford Canal. There were two hotel boats, Jupiter and Saturn. I was in the one with the engine and Ernie was in the towed butty boat.

The plan was to journey from Oxford to Warwick where we were to explore the castle, but because the authorities had not been informed of our two boats coming they had withdrawn the pumps up to Cropredy lock and we ran aground!

Ernie and I got to know each other as we walked ahead of the boats to set the locks. He told me that a rather sad lady on his boat had seen me with a half-bottle of rosé wine at the evening meal (the remainder went into the fridge for the next day)! She had pointed out to him my wickedness and he had found this highly amusing.

Ernie and Eileen, both in their forties, married and embarked on a very happy life together. At 18 Ernie had been called up and posted to Korea where he had been badly injured. When he came home he didn't want to be shut up indoors in a factory or office, and had a variety of jobs including those of milkman and security guard.

When I first met Ernie he had jet black hair and beautiful brown eyes full of laughter, surrounded by laughter lines. He was tall and well-built with wonderful hands. He was the eldest of 10 siblings. His mother was a gentle ladylike little person who was dominated by her noisy overbearing husband.

Ernie was a gentle person of simple needs with a wonderful sense of fun, like a small boy at times. He could always make me laugh. We never had any money to spare but even when he was out of work for a year we paid the mortgage regularly and never got into debt.

*

Both Sylvia and Eileen noted an unusual amount of interference with electrical gadgetry when they were newly bereaved.

Here is Sylvia's experience:

Immediately following Jim's passing, I experienced a very difficult problem with the central-locking system of my car. On one occasion, while attending an outpatient appointment at the local hospital, I found it impossible to lock the car. In order not to miss the appointment I had to leave the car unlocked with my little dog inside. Jim and I were devoted (I still am) to this dog, Tim - a Tibetan Lhasa Apso. Tim had been Jim's therapy as he became more and more ill. I was so worried something might happen to him while I was inside the hospital that I asked every available security man and porter to keep an eye out for him Thankfully, when I returned to the car, Tim was safe.

The problem continued and I had three visits within one week from different RAC men. None of them could detect the problem. However, on the third visit the officer said, despairingly, "I think you've got a ghost in that car!" Of course, he had no idea what had happened to me. Later, when in a workshop, the car was found to have a very rare problem somewhere in the steering column.

A few days before Jim's funeral I had a visit from a friend who had been close to him for many years. Whilst we were talking about Jim the lights suddenly fused. My friend traced the problem to the summerhouse where some years earlier he had fixed shelving for Jim's large collection of books. Jim used the summerhouse as a place to write.

For some weeks I continued to have many problems with the lighting in our home – problems that couldn't be accounted for. In desperation one evening I was joined by Angela Howard and, having lit a candle, we spoke to Jim telling him everything was safe, he had no need to worry about anything and we asked him to solve the problems with the lighting. From that time onwards the lighting problems ceased.

These experiences made me feel Jim was finding it difficult to adjust – maybe he didn't want to leave me and Tim. As part of my spiritual belief, I had always felt that there was a life after our time on Earth, but I had never expected to be convinced so soon after Jim passed on.

Here is Eileen's experience:

I was aware of phenomena in the house. I saw hazy shadows and movement out of the corner of my eye. The light bulbs were fluctuating and I was having to replace blown bulbs frequently but I knew that there was no problem with the electricity. It only happened in the living room and kitchen, and only in the room that I was in at the time.

Several times in shops the till would malfunction and once when a cashier had been rude to me, her till just closed down as she finished serving me and she had to be moved to another desk as the technician could not get it working again. That was the first time I really laughed. I knew that Ernie was there protecting me. Shop alarms would go off as I walked out which I found really amusing. At Christmas time I had arranged for Ernie's name to be put on a tree of remembrance in the church at Rye and I went there to visit. On this occasion the alarm went off as I walked <u>into</u> a shop.

One night I was awoken by the telephone ringing. I could

hear a strange sound but no voice. I thought that it was a nuisance call but afterwards realised that the sound reminded me of the oxygen machine that Ernie was using when he passed. No number was recorded but the time was 4.55 am. I wish that I had had the courage to ask who was calling.

Another time I was very stupidly standing on a chair doing something to the shed in the garden when I tipped over backwards and should have landed with my head on the rockery. I can only describe my fall as cushioned. I was unhurt. Another time I fell in the street and my ring was crushed into my finger yet I did not have a bruise.

Now that I have energy-saving bulbs they do not fluctuate, but Ernie plays with the video. One day as I watched a film the counter was going backwards but the film was going forwards.

Three years running now the alarm on my battery-operated clock has gone off at 7am on New Year's morning. Ernie also seems to be able to affect my watch which will stop and start again especially during periods of meditation.

*

These experiences are, in fact, very common at times of transition. In his book *Life Beyond Death. What Should We Expect*, David Fontana writes:

Another ADC (after death communication) reported relatively frequently these days is the perplexing behaviour of electrical devices. Sometimes vacuum cleaners, radios, televisions or light bulbs regularly switch themselves on and off, even though they are checked and rechecked and no fault is found. The case for paranormality is increased if these inexplicable events follow a distinct pattern. For example, the deceased's reading lamp may come on around the time he/she was in the habit of switching it on, or it may blink on and off as if in greeting at certain times.

Here at the cottage, the landing light and the bathroom light blink repeatedly at times, sometimes for a period of ten seconds or more after being switched on. They then settle down and give normal steady light. This has happened ever since Martin died. I have never changed the bulbs as they are long-life ones, and anyway I rather enjoy the phenomenon.

Once, years ago, after I'd received a phone call telling me of the expected death of an elderly aunt, I experienced my radio being turned on as I sat quietly taking in the news. Years later, when I was visiting a friend whose partner had recently died, we both jumped as the door bell rang. He'd been explaining to me that all sorts of electrical phenomena were happening in the house including the door bell ringing. We both went to the door and when he opened it there was no-one there.

*

Both Sylvia and Eileen longed for communication with their husbands, just as I did. Sylvia went to see Paul Lambillion at the end of January 2008 just six weeks after Jim had died.

Early in my first visit to Paul he became aware of Jim's presence and a number of extraordinary links and revelations were made. Jim said how much he missed me but said my 'ticket was not printed yet' and that I've got to 'hang around for a bit longer'. I explained to Paul that Jim had once been a bus conductor – a very happy time in his early life.

"I heard the song, 'Swing on the bell, Nelly', about five minutes ago!" said Paul, and so the link was made with Jim's ticket remark.

Jim referred to his favourite hobby of playing bowls and

Paul turned to me asking what a bias was. There was then a three-way discussion, as though Jim was sitting in the room, as to the meaning of the word in the context of bowls. With Jim's help it was established that the 'bias' was a piece of metal which enabled the 'wood' to curve. I felt this was a totally convincing example of mediumistic communication, as this was a fact unknown to either Paul or me.

My parents and an aunt, Cath, who was always very close, also came 'to meet me', and Paul asked if I had my aunt's name in a Bible or prayer book. I have. My aunt referred to some special china of hers which I have, and then gave me some advice on nutrition and my health, which was typical of her. She had been a vegetarian cook and had lectured on nutrition in the 1940s. She was way ahead of her time.

My mother referred to a beautiful piece of embroidery of hers which I have, and my father was very much present, organising everyone and demonstrating his knowledge and skill as a gardener.

There were other convincing pieces of communication, and Jim reflected on his long illness and brought me a bunch of flowers including roses, his favourite flowers, as a thank you gift for caring for him.

I will never forget the degree of comfort I gained from this first meeting with Paul. Although I couldn't see Jim, I knew he was closer to me than ever.

*

Eileen writes:

Ernie and I had become interested in colour healing and crystals, and I had bought a book written by the medium Betty

Shine. I sent her a letter and a copy of his photograph and received a standard letter but with a loving personal handwritten message which I found very helpful.

Eileen found a reference to the College of Psychic Studies in Betty Shine's book and eventually, six months after Ernie died, she made an appointment for a sitting with a medium.

February 2001. I shall never forget the first meeting with Kathryn Hall, six months after Ernie died. I was terrified and, as I had time to spare, walked around the block several times before I was brave enough to walk up the steps and into the College. As I walked in I felt comfortable and warm. People in the reception area were so <u>normal</u>. I suppose that my idea of a medium had been influenced by Margaret Rutherford in Blithe Spirit, *or visions of Victorian style séances.*

I was sent up to a bright, plain room and standing in front of the window with the winter sunlight streaming through was a young woman. There were two chairs and a table on which was a pink crystal and a candle.

Kathryn was aware that Ernie had walked through the door with me and was standing behind me. She was amazed that this had happened so quickly, as usually people take longer to adjust. She said that he had prepared for his death as if by route map, and accurately described his passing. She said she now knew who had blown a light bulb in her flat the previous evening and described him as a friendly poltergeist doing tricks to amuse me. She found him to be funny and very loving. He did not pass on to me the secrets of the universe but was more concerned that my back was cold at night against an outside wall and wanted me to move the bed and get a new mattress... Kathryn mentioned Ernie's once errant brother by name and said that he was now very happy. He had been married a few weeks before. She mentioned a favourite uncle who had passed and whom Ernie had met again.

At this time, Eileen writes, she had very unpleasant neighbours who were making her life difficult. They wanted to force her to move so that they could buy her house.

Ernie was very angry that I was being so unkindly treated at home and wanted me to move. Kathryn said that I have a long life ahead of me and he wants me to be fit to enjoy this. She said I was going to be very happy and have many real friends. This part I found very hard to accept as I was reclusive and hated being in groups of people. She was correct but it took a long time to achieve.

It was an hour-long sitting and I have it on tape. She mentioned names which I did not understand at the time, though much of the information now makes sense. I regret that I cannot tell Ernie's family, but his favourite niece is maturing into a very understanding young woman and I may be able to tell her when the time is right.

*

Evidence of how closely our loved ones are following our progress here on Earth is also given by Sylvia as she describes how Jim was aware of her struggle to carry forward her complaint that he had suffered medical negligence in the final weeks of his life. In April 2009 she had another session with Paul:

After Paul and I had had an initial chat, he said that Jim was standing behind me cleaning his glasses with a handkerchief! He had been reading through the papers relating to his medical neglect case. He said one or two people have 'butterflies', talked about a cover-up, and said he felt sure there was professional mismanagement. Jim also added that he knew I was bringing the case not to take revenge but to try to ensure that such things don't happen again. The case has been difficult and protracted and I had been working flat out on it. Listening to Jim's words, it felt as though he had been working with me as all my actions and attitudes had been exactly as he described.

For many reasons, and with great reluctance, I was unable to keep Jim at home till the end. He had been suffering from Parkinson's Disease (accompanied latterly by Lewy Body Dementia), asbestos related lung disease and other complications for several years. Whilst in the nursing home he suffered medical neglect, as his form of dementia was not understood. Although I spent many hours each day with him, the situation grew worse. However, palliative care and healing from a local church minister finally helped him to a peaceful end.

Two months after Jim's funeral I decided I had to lodge a formal complaint with our local authority regarding the neglect. I did this to try and prevent such a situation happening again, so that Jim's suffering had not been in vain.

For the last year, as I have journeyed through the official complaints procedure, I have had to relive many times the trauma of Jim's last days. Fairly early in the process the local authority upheld five, and partially upheld two, of the nine elements of the complaint. One was judged to be inconclusive and one was not upheld.

Nearly every evening since Jim passed, Tim has been very disturbed by a 'presence' in our home that I have been unable to see. This has happened either in our sitting room or in the bedroom. I have just tried to reassure him. He was very close to Jim and grieved deeply when he was no longer here.

During the night of the third/fourth February 2009, an extraordinary occurrence took place. I suddenly woke up to find Tim jumping around on my bed (he normally sleeps soundly)

Martin speaking to an Esperanto group in Poland. Late 1980s

Celebrating our Silver Wedding anniversary, November, 2001. Paris, on a boat trip down the Seine.

Alison Parkes of Colchester Meeting brought Lorna and her friends for a pottery party to celebrate Lorna's 8th birthday, 2000

Lorna showing us what she's making. Martin in his element!

Three generations of the Howard family, Martin, Mike and Nathan, on Martin's favourite seat by the pond at Webb's Cottage, July 2003

The view of the cottage from the seat by the pond, June 2009

Martin's funeral, 30th December, 2003. The coffin on the bier with family and friends gathered round. Mike is in the foreground in a brown jacket. Tim is playing a guitar with Claudie beside him wearing a hat. Becky is the other side of Tim. I am behind Mike

The pottery which eventually became a little house called 'Martins', May 2009

Paul Lambillion, cracking a joke! Very typical! July 2009

Paul and a group of his students, July 2009

Sylvia and Jim in their early years together

Sylvia, Jim and Timmy, 2004

Eileen and Ernie's wedding day, 20th April, 1981

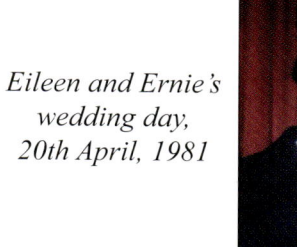

Ernie's 20th wedding anniversary present of twenty yellow roses (given to Eileen by Kathryn) complete with red admiral butterfly, April 2001

Ernie with a friend - he loved animals

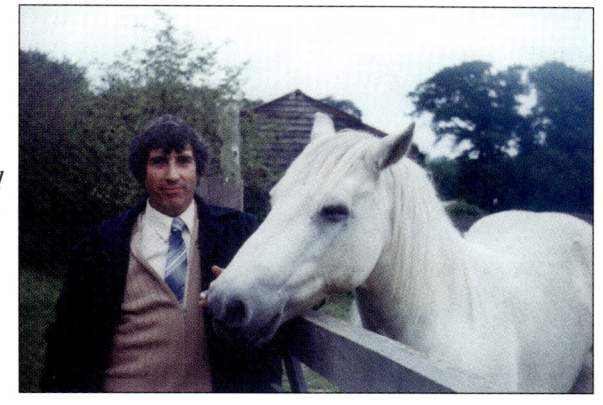

My friend-next-door, Margaret Koolman, who supported us both through Martin's illness, and me through the years that followed his death

Prue, who could "see" Martin and my father at the cottage

Nova, who arrived in the village just after Martin's diagnosis and became our loving companion

and standing in the doorway the unmistakeable image of my husband. Until that time I had been sleeping soundly as I usually manage to do. On 4th February I was to face a panel at County Hall in Chelmsford, as part of the complaints procedure. I am convinced that Jim wanted me to be aware of his support and had showed it in this visible manner. This was so much in keeping with his kind nature.

In this session I described the experience to Paul and he gave the following explanation, which I have summarised.

When our loved ones try to connect with us they have to use our imagination. The imagination is the tool of the spirit and it operates between two glands in the head (the pineal and the pituitary). The Ancients understood this. People connecting with us from another level have to first connect with our imagination, and then they help us to focus on a projection of themselves as we would remember them. In certain moments, when we're tired or not well, or when our physical resistance is low, we're more able mentally and emotionally to tap into their thoughts. We can feel their presence, we may even see them.

When we're no longer in the physical body we're not limited in space and time as we are here. Jim was probably aware of my thoughts and was able to focus himself in that space for a while at another level which I was sensitive enough to see. And he didn't disappear. My awareness of him suddenly went.

Eileen tells of an experience she had on a later visit to Kathryn.

In April 2001, I made another appointment with Kathryn. It was close to the date that would have been our 20th wedding anniversary and this seemed a good way to mark the day. Kathryn's appointments were made by the College receptionist and she had no idea who was going to walk through the door. As

I walked in she was pleased to see me and said Ernie was there with me. She said that she saw so many people in the course of her work that she could not remember their names but that he had shown her Morecambe and Wise. She said that Ernie wanted me to buy a video player so that I could watch films that would make me laugh, and so that he could enjoy them as well. He said he knew I was useless with modern technology but that I only had to press the PLAY button.

I was more confident this time and knew what to expect! It was amazing that questions that I had been asking Ernie were answered, and I was given an intimation of my future psychic development, which at the time seemed highly improbable.

The sitting this time was a happy reunion with Ernie in which he spoke of spending time with his dear mother. He warned me that the negative energy of my own mother was around me and had to be excluded. I have since had communication with my maternal grandmother and great-grandmother who also find my mother a very difficult lady, but they are pleased that they produced me.

Before Kathryn closed down she said that there was something that she had to tell me before I left. On her table this time had been a beautiful bouquet of yellow rosebuds which she said she had been impelled to buy on her way to the College that morning. Ernie's last message was that the roses were for me. There were 20 yellow roses. All my rooms are painted primrose yellow. Ever since Ernie died I have tried to keep yellow flowers to his memory on the kitchen windowsill. Red roses, though very nice, would have had no special significance, but to be given 20 yellow roses just a few days after our 20th anniversary, for me had the WOW factor.

I took several photographs of the roses indoors, but one lovely sunny afternoon I took them out into the garden and as

I did so a beautiful butterfly settled on them. I stood in wonder looking at this perfect butterfly. I went indoors to get my camera and to my amazement the lovely creature was still there and remained until after I had taken a series of photographs when it flew away. I did not see another butterfly until July.

Eileen received the gift of roses. Sylvia now tells how she has been collecting feathers.

Feathers! Nearly a hundred of them – mostly white! A few months after Jim's passing I decided to visit an experienced lady medium who lived locally and whose work was highly regarded. During my time with her she said I would be aware of feathers and since that moment I have! It seems that one will always be placed very strategically in my path when I am very happy, very sad, or am worried about a problem. I have collected all these feathers and they are gradually filling a small basket which I have next to my bed. The medium told me they represent angels. I really do believe this as every time I see a feather I experience a warm and happy feeling as I pick it up. It is always a great comfort.

When I asked Paul how this could happen he had no ready answer but confirmed that it often did. He said it was difficult to know exactly how it occurred but that he saw it as a sign of reassurance to us. I certainly feel this very much each time a feather is placed in my path.

*

Jim's continuing care for Sylvia is shown in this extract from the session in April, 2009.

Jim encouraged me to play the piano, which I haven't done for some time. "He's put a piano keyboard in front of you with 'Come on Sparky!'" Paul said. Behind Jim's laughter I believe he was trying to help me move on. Let me explain. Heaped on the piano are bags of sympathy cards relating to his passing and also his birthday cards – his 80th birthday took place just a few months before he passed. I really need to sort through these, clear the piano and then begin playing. There's another connection. I have a little jewellery box that sits on our dressing-table. It's in the shape of a grand piano and when wound up and opened it plays **Solveig's Song** *by Grieg. We bought it on holiday in Norway where we visited Grieg's home.*

At this point I found myself still asking the question 'How can I cope?' Paul said in reply, "Jim said you would move forward in life. There is something growing in us all the time." Paul added: "Even when we think we're static we're not. There's something growing and changing in us all the time. Often we move forward more in the moments we feel blocked than when it's all flowing. You can't not grow."

Jim felt I should have cleared up his belongings by June 21st (the Solstice, in fact). Paul continued, "There may be some important news about the case by then." Quoting Jim, Paul said, "To let go of the feelings, you have to let go of the things. It's the clutter that's holding you back more than the case." But he added "I'll come and haunt you. You won't get rid of me!" And he also said, that in order to let go I must try and speed up the case.

Jim went into another less serious phase with singing and more references to food. I often used to make my own rice puddings and he said he would be 'sniffing one'. I think this was to encourage me to cook for myself which I am finding difficult.

The care was typical of Jim but this session also had its hilarious moments.

I was feeling particularly low at this time and finding it difficult to cope without him, but this session was just what I was needing, and each time I replay the cassette recording it's impossible not to join in the laughter. Throughout there were jokes and snatches of old songs that Jim knew and loved. There is a strong sense of empathy between Jim and Paul, and Paul says he is sure they would have got on well if they had known each other in life. Both had been Butlins' Red Coats at some time in their younger years: 'paid to make people laugh'!

As Paul struggled to understand what he was hearing he suddenly burst into an amusing old song, 'Right, said Fred', which is about two men who keep having tea breaks while they are supposed to be working. I felt Jim was linking his sense of humour with his awareness of my liking for a cup of tea. The humour continued for a while and then Jim turned his attention to our small but pretty garden. I had been pruning roses for the spring but Jim had noticed a new standard rose that my children had given me that was still waiting to be pruned. Jim had a great passion for roses and told me to trim it with great care.

Jim mentioned a lady named Tricia who I had recently had lunch with. She had been one of his carers and he asked me to give her his regards when I next see her.

Off into humour again. Jim talked about Thomas the Tank Engine and said how he had loved steam trains. He remembered Tenterden in Kent, a place where he knew another Tricia and which also has a steam railway, so combining two memories. Paul then said that Jim had put on an old-fashioned train-driver's hat. He said he had always dreamed of being a fireman on a steam train!

This session was becoming very fast moving and varied. It seemed to me that Jim was wanting to make the most of this precious time together and talk to me about many subjects, all of which he knew I would connect with him.

The next few moments were very special and emotional as Jim told Paul he had his mother with him. He had met her since he arrived and said it was great to make contact with her. He didn't know her very well as she had died when he was only seven. She was his <u>real</u> mother. He was very lucky, he said, because he had two mothers in a sense – his birth mother and his wonderful step-mother.

My mother then appeared with some rock cakes and doing her knitting. She was gifted in many areas of craft and cooking.

Paul could then hear Ken Dodd's well-known song Happiness. *Jim would often sing this song, so this was very evidential. He was holding up a picture of Ken Dodd and his tickling stick. I was to get a copy of the song and if ever I was 'down in the dumps' I was to play it and it would make me think of him as I did my dusting ' up with the cobwebs'. This was completely convincing. Jim was a very happy man and always did his best to make others happy. Bless his heart – he hasn't changed at all!*

More humour followed when Paul asked me if I had my father's watch. I said "no, but I have Jim's" – which I was wearing. Paul said "Sorry, Jim, I got that wrong." This was followed by great laughter from Paul as he said Jim folded his arms (joking, of course) and said "I wasn't her ruddy father!"

"You're bringing him alive for me!" I told Paul.

<u>My</u> mother came through again but then, almost simultaneously, Paul heard the music of 42nd Street! *Paul said, "It's like a cabaret turn here today!" My mother was still making cakes and Jim was enjoying them! This was an extremely poignant part of the session for me because my mother left this Earth when she was only fifty-six and I was twenty-two. Her death was very unexpected and sudden, and was a tragedy for*

myself and my dear father. I will always remember the brave way in which he coped with this period of his life. It has therefore been a great comfort for me to have these close connections with my mother.

Jim made reference to us coming together in later life by saying "it was a short time but it was a good time." He said he wished it could have been longer but "it was worth it, despite all the hassle."

The session concluded in a most evidential way. Suddenly, according to Paul, Jim put on a woman's wig whilst Paul could see a L'Oreal advertisement being shown. Jim kept repeating "I am worth it! Because you're worth it!"

I almost fell off my chair at this point! Towards the end of his life Jim used to be very amused by this TV advert and was always jokingly saying to me and to his carers "Because you're worth it!" This, for me, was Jim suddenly coming alive again. Paul commented that this was good evidence.

Paul's final comment. "Jim makes a strong effort and is keen to make a connection."

I left this sitting feeling more uplifted than ever before. I feel Jim is with me night and day, guiding and comforting me constantly. After a sitting like this there is no room for doubt. I just <u>know</u> there is some form of afterlife.

... Although every day continues to be a mental and physical struggle, I gain immense comfort from playing the recordings of meetings in which Jim has given me messages through Paul Lambillion.

After Ernie's death Eileen followed a path which eventually led her to Quakerism. It was a pathway which began during Ernie's lifetime, and Kathryn was able to see how it would unfold.

On the Saturday after his death, I went to Rye in Sussex as I had promised him I would. In hospital we pretended that we were on the beach and like the Teletubby he would grin and say 'run away'. It was lonely without him, of course, but I felt close to him there as it had been one of our favourite haunts. I went to the old church on top of the hill and in the book shop I bought two cards. On one was an extract by William Penn which I later discovered in Quaker Faith and Practice *(22.95). It was like greeting an old friend. The other begins 'Death is nothing at all', by Henry Scott Holland. I went to the tea shop we had visited in the previous May, our last time together in Rye, and was warmly greeted by the owner who gave me a pot of coffee and a big bear hug. I really needed that and am so grateful to him for his kindness to me that day. It is a precious memory.*

It was at a later sitting that Kathryn suggested that I went to a Quaker Meeting, and saw me in summer sitting by a duck pond. Several months later I wandered into Harpenden Meeting (Eric Morecambe's wife still lives in the village!) and eventually became a member. Yes, there is a duck pond on the common just a stone's throw from the Meeting House.

Ernie would have loved Quaker Meetings. He had great respect for Quakerism and would always remark if we went past the Luton Meeting House about the ambulance driver in Korea who drove him to the MASH, who was a Quaker. One Good Friday we saw the film Friendly Persuasion *on TV and he was very moved by this and again extolled the bravery of the ambulance man. I realise that we had bought several bits of Quaker literature. I wish now that it was something that we had done together years ago but I am sure that he has led me in this direction.*

Finally, an update from Eileen on the way her life has developed, and an interesting remark from an electrician.

The attitude of my neighbours has improved since I have become involved more with community matters and I realize that what is important is not what I do, but <u>who</u> knows me (some fairly important members of the Islamic community). So now I am safe and <u>almost</u> respected.

I was impelled to watch TV one evening a few weeks ago and to my amazement it was a programme about 'Saturn', the narrow boat that Ernie was on when we first met. It has been restored to its original condition and is a rare historical vessel. I am convinced that he wanted me to see this, and can now communicate directly.

At Christmas last year I was having a difficult time due to proposed building repairs and needing to sort through and clear 'memory stuff'. The light in the kitchen became very strange and kept going out, so I thought that I had a wiring problem - one of the areas to be checked and repaired.

When the electrician investigated he found no fault with the wiring and the light has shown no problem since. He could not understand the effect that I described until I mentioned 'spirit' interaction. He was pleased with this explanation and said it could be the reason. He often comes across this phenomenon!

Ernie had made himself present.

Chapter 11

Experiencing bereavement

This is not an easy chapter to write. In fact, knowing that I would have to re-live this part of my life was probably a major factor in delaying the writing of this book.

If it is painful to write, it may also be painful to read. Sometimes though, if you are experiencing pain yourself, it is good to know that others have travelled the same road and survived. If you have had a recent bereavement my heart goes out to you. I hope you have loving support around you. If you do not have it in the physical world then you can be assured that, whether you are aware of it or not, loving helpers *are* reaching out to you from the spiritual world. Try reaching out to them if you can, however difficult that may seem.

As I have said, I wrote every day in my diary, even the day Martin died. This may sound odd, but to me it was helpful, almost essential. At times my mind and emotions were in turmoil. I couldn't separate thoughts from feelings. And I couldn't control them.

Grief washed me up in some strange places. This is what I wrote six days after his death.

Saturday, December 27th, 2003

It's as if a mould has been made of a relief map and placed upside down with muddy water in it. The Pit. It is full of troughs and peaks and hollows. Water rolls me around it, helpless. I fetch up in some place I can't scramble out of and I lie, limbs all anywhere, exhausted, and experience what's there. It may be comforting or it may be painful with unfinished things. Sometimes I am grieving for the whole, strong Martin as he was before he became ill. Then the waste in ordinary Earthly terms becomes unbearable – all his knowledge and power to do good things, gone. But often I am seeing the Martin whose body was becoming more and more distressing to be in. Then I am so relieved, almost euphoric, that he is out of it and exploring in his wonderful new body, places which will be full of wonder for him. Then again, <u>how is he?</u> Is he full of regret for leaving here? Is he full of excitement for the new life? Perhaps both.

Sunday, December 28th, 2003

The best place to wash up in is the place where I am relieved that Martin is free of suffering. There, I am with the image of Martin in his uncomfortable body, as it had become in the end. And then the wonderful feeling of release, like a space rocket leaving Earth, and suddenly the pain, discomfort, the loss of hearing also, are jettisoned as this beautiful new body, completely strong and healthy goes shooting out of the old one...

On the same day I was writing about another aspect of my experience.

I am aware of a <u>process</u>. At the back of my mind there are small wheels gently turning, I can almost hear them whirring, and I'm not quite sure what it is they are doing but it's part of a necessary, almost mechanical, process – that's the only word for it. As I drove along in the car I thought I would listen to a radio programme. It had to be a suitable one. It was Boxing Day and there was a quiz on Woman's Hour. *That was fine. It suited me. Small bits of concentration. Not a story I had to engage in. No* emotion. Mental stimulation and fun. But I had to negotiate with the wheels to see if it was OK to turn them off for a while. I felt slightly guilty that I was going to divert my attention from them. It was important to come back and start them up again in the place where they had left off. This is a very strong feeling. What on earth it is I don't know. It isn't a process of separation exactly but of reconstitution.

Another image I remember having of this process was of hands gently folding pieces of fine cloth, endlessly folding, folding, and then laying them away in drawers with tissue paper. I suppose that for the months before Martin died, out of fear and exhaustion, I hadn't dared to think. Now there was filing to be done. I can't explain it but can only say that it happened.

It seemed important to chronicle everything. I wrote:

There are so many facets to mourning - which is different from grief. I mourn the loss of Martin as a partner, not exactly spiritually, mentally, emotionally, but certainly physically, and the others reconstituted in a new form. The partnership is still there but it's different. I am taking the first teetering steps forward in the material world as one, instead of half a couple. I feel like a toddler. I have no-one with whom to hold the very intimate dialogue and chat anymore – the continuous conversation which breaks off and reforms at each mealtime and meeting through the day. I talk to different people - lots of them - and they speak to me very lovingly and are close up emotionally but they are <u>several</u> and they all have different memories. The last months have been a campaign to overcome the cancer: the pain, the discomfort. To keep the diet and the treatments going. All the strategies we used to keep spirits up. The tiny little things we shared through the nights and days that no-one else knew about. There is no need to cope anymore. I am not the hugely necessary coping partner. Martin used frequently to thank me for all the help I was giving him. Now he doesn't need me in that way. Thank goodness, as I was running out of strategies. It feels as if no-one needs me. I want to crawl into a warm, dark hole and just be a resting, hibernating creature.

I'm rambling. Mentally I seem to have blinkers on, trying to do one thing at a time but not having reliable all-round vision. I may forget something huge, be very rude to someone, unintentionally, by forgetting something they've done – a letter or card received. No, I am not functioning normally. Like someone drunk I may think my reactions are OK, but they may not be.

To return to the different things I mourn. Loss of partner in the material, everyday world. Loss of the future as we'd seen it and mapped it out. Loss of Martin's joy in his pottery, garden, home. Just two days before he died he was saying how he loved his home and couldn't think of anywhere better to be. And at last, before his illness, he seemed idyllically happy. Loss of this is the loss of a beautiful and powerful joy carrying us, as if in double harness, into the future. A power and a joy which lifts the heart because the one I love is so happy and I am so happy for him. Everything was good and worthwhile, exciting, uplifting. Now I have to remake a different future with only my own energy. Can I be bothered?

His retirement which he had worked hard for, and earned. Gone.

*

Grief is something which happens to us, mourning is something we do. The hands laying away memories that I had been aware of are part of the mourning process. Being hurled around the pit is grief. It's hell, but, being watery, it does fluctuate. There are moments of respite, when the currents subside. Little flashes of relief and humour. Joy, even.

What I didn't write in my diary but can clearly remember feeling at this time was the sensation of having lost a part of my body. My right arm, in fact. I knew how the loss of a limb changes the centre of gravity in a body. I have stood at a bedside and watched a person take their first tentative steps with the aid of crutches after losing a leg. First they must just stand - for however long it takes to get the new sense of balance. An arm or a leg forms a considerable proportion of the body weight so muscles need to adjust and compensate. In the early days after the loss of Martin everything felt so strange, it seemed that there was the real possibility of falling flat on my face. A very strange *physical* feeling. We need to be *upheld*, literally, and this is what others can do for us through their thoughts and prayers as well as in practical ways.

The daily obstacles the world presents have to be negotiated in a new way. And, to use a rather gruesome metaphor, the amputation wound is raw. When it brushes against the crasser elements of the outer world it hurts. When a bereaved person is well supported by others, as I was, many of these inevitable blows are cushioned and delayed, but sooner or later they still have to be faced.

And I was busy in the outer world, which was a blessing at times but at others felt so draining I hardly knew how to carry on. I was Monthly Meeting Clerk and also Clerk of Quaker Fellowship for Afterlife Studies (about which more in chapter 14). I was active in the group I had co-founded some years ago, which records plays for hospital radio, and other organisations. During Martin's illness I had been writing a comedy, which was a great escape for me, and in the January and February of 2004 we were rehearsing and recording it.

And yet, I often felt a fear of setting foot outside my home because the world seemed so alien and threatening. Sometimes I felt so confused and inadequate I couldn't remember anything, and thought I might lose my keys or my head - *"Just put one foot in front of the other!"* There were places to visit which we last visited as a couple. As I was now living alone there was the realisation that if I was away from home there was no-one there to return to, or to phone if I needed help. No Martin to phone me if I was staying away for any length of time.

There were the continual letters arriving addressed to the two of us. Small blows. (Letters addressed to Martin continued to come for several years.) There were fears that I couldn't manage to talk sensibly to solicitors, accountants, or deal with machines, or change a light bulb. All these anxieties can pile up and seem huge, and you are a child and the tears come. I still walk round the central heating boiler as if it is a dangerous animal. I don't think Martin understood its little ways either but at least I felt he could read the instruction manual with intelligence if need be!

I tottered through days and parts of days feeling unfocused and even partially brain-dead, but there were also times when I thought I was functioning rather well. We have public faces and private faces. I would often hear my voice talking quite sensibly 'out there', while inside I felt a quivering wreck. Dressing tidily and having my hair and face looking reasonable were a great help. They supported my image and enabled me to present myself to the world with dignity. Sometimes my public face could perform for long periods of time, but in the end I would return home to sit in a heap, rest and try to recover. Convalesce. For hours. Recovering from the loss of a partner definitely feels like convalescence after major illness.

Day and night were not clearly defined either, they leaked into one another wearily. My sleep pattern was odd. I would have hours of wakefulness in the darkness and long naps in the daytime with the curtains drawn against the light.

There is no way round this process, one can only go through it. It is the price we pay for the joy of having had a loving relationship.

*

I had tremendous help from family and friends, particularly my friend, Margaret, who was right next door. I was fortunate. And night and morning, and sometimes during the night, I played a wonderful cassette recorded by Paul Lambillion called *Gently and Deeply*. It encourages relaxation through breathing, and supports through positive affirmations. There are visualisations accompanied by musical sounds, and the whole tape which runs for about 20 minutes is incredibly life-affirming and reassuring. It seems to say 'all is well', ultimately, underneath are the everlasting arms, and all is well.

Despite being tempest-tossed by my thoughts and emotions I never actually despaired of eventually coming through. I knew I hadn't 'lost' Martin. What I was suffering was the actual physical loss of him as a daily companion and partner, but I had a strong belief that our souls remained linked and that contact would be maintained at that level whether I was aware of it or not.

*

Other people's unhelpful reactions were often painful. If you have had a major bereavement you will probably have encountered the person who is sadly lacking in tact. Not long after Martin died I went into the local library. I was still at the stage of blundering about and feeling very vulnerable. I was also aware that I was conducting a bit of an experiment for others who might be in the same situation. I simply asked innocently if there was a section on bereavement?

The librarian I spoke to was a woman of a similar same age to myself. There was an imperceptible intake of breath and she took a step back as if I had a contagious disease. I can't remember exactly what she said but it was in hushed tones and sounded a bit wobbly. Maybe she'd been bereaved herself, or maybe she feared she might be. Undoubtedly she felt vulnerable too.

She directed me to the upper floor, where a younger woman reacted more professionally to my enquiry. She took me on a tour of the relevant areas of the library and explained that the books were scattered about in sections such as 'counselling and self help' and 'illness' and that there would be a lot in 'biography' – Gloria Hunniford's *Next to You* and Sheila Hancock's *The Two of Us*, for example.

This scattered approach isn't actually much use! A bereaved person is in a state where a large notice - BEREAVEMENT - would be helpful to stumble towards. Only large notices and clear words really penetrate the fog that the brain tends to be in much of the time. It's probably best if books are put into the hands of the bereaved by kind friends who know them really well and can choose carefully. The right book can be a godsend. A companion. The voice of someone who has suffered and come through. And, because the brain is so numb, a book is invaluable to read and re-read and pick up in the night for a bit of comfort. I have seen books of this kind which were so thumbed they fell to pieces. A friend of mine, after losing her husband, clung to a *file of paper* given her by someone who had devotedly photocopied the pages of a disintegrated, out of print book.

*

In the minds of some people, loss of my partner made me an object of pity and of fear. A symbol of something they dreaded. I think it's best to face head-on that this is so. It wasn't new to me because it's something life teaches you, and also I'd been a bereavement visitor and a counsellor and talked to many people suffering loss.

The way to deal with it, if you are able, is to firmly tell yourself that the problem is *theirs*. They are not actually seeing *you,* they are seeing themselves as they would not wish to be. Their own pain is simply too acute and they cannot get away from you or change the subject fast enough. Sometimes this makes them very clumsy.

Soon after my mother died I remember meeting a neighbour when I was out walking my dog. He fell in beside me briefly, obviously feeling he ought to say something.

"Funeral over?" he asked tentatively.

"Yes."

He seemed relieved. "Oh, well that's all right then," he said briskly, as if, once the mortal remains were laid to rest, life automatically returned to normal and no more need be said!

It's painful but it's *their* problem. Somehow realising this and realising also that they are going to have to come to terms with loss in their own lives, sooner or later, makes it bearable. Or it did to me - some of the time. Well, it depended how I was feeling!

And I'm sure I've done it myself! In my younger years *I've* crossed the road to avoid speaking to someone who I knew was bereaved. I simply didn't know what to say. You don't! And I'm *still* not sure what the right thing is. It's probably different for everyone. And you don't want to risk putting your foot in it. And you don't want to make someone, who is out in public soon after a major loss, break down. Or so our cultural background tells us. Say something kind and sympathetic, in the middle of the high street and the tears may flow! And *then* what will both of you do?

Platitudes are awful. 'Time will heal', 'he's gone to a better place', 'it was a merciful release', 'he had a good life'. They're all true in their way but when trotted out with a little smile and a pat on the arm they can stab like a dagger.

When babies die, people are apt to say 'you can have another one' or 'well, what a good thing you've got other children' - if you have. When my niece lost a baby she wrote an article about the reactions she received and what might, in some cases, have been a more helpful approach.

After Martin died, a close friend who is a healer and counsels many people, simply asked me "How do you help someone who has been bereaved?" I still don't know if she was *really* asking for guidance or if this was her way of helping me – knowing how I like giving advice! I think it was a very clever thing to do.

We talked for some time and in the end agreed that the most important thing to give is time. A willingness to slow down and listen and *enter into the grief.* High street encounters *are* difficult and I think always will be. I was actually glad when some people *did* cross over to avoid me. As well as not knowing what to say to a bereaved person, as a bereaved person myself I often didn't know what to say back. You can be brief – 'Oh, coping,', 'not too bad, thank you', that sort of thing, or you can launch into a long description of what has happened and of your feelings. Personally, I found long conversations with people I was not particularly close to, draining.

'Adjusting.' This seemed quite a useful word in some

situations, if a bit clinical.

Some may welcome any chance to talk, but I was pouring out my feelings to my diary and those close to me, and I found first contacts with people I knew less well were often formalities to be got through with difficulty. I hope I was polite. People mean well but can easily crush one.

Avoidance may continue. This is one of the sadder aspects of the loss of a partner. Friends who are couples may drop away. A bereaved person is a threat, a sad reminder, an odd number, a bit of a puzzle. Probably people who take this attitude are not really worth bothering with. *Again, it's their problem.* And there are a lot of single people out there to meet and share with, who will have a greater understanding of life and a greater depth of character from having come through the experience of loss.

*

The first year seemed to be full of anniversaries and special dates which brought memories flooding in. I remember living quite as much in the past as the present. Also there are the first times of visiting people or places on your own, and the realization that you bring sadness to those people however much you try not to. You arrive and greet friends as positively as you can on that particular day, but a sort of miasma often seems to descend which can plunge the occasion into gloom. I think the answer is for friends to try and remain in the present, rather than think about what has been lost.

It's important to welcome a person as themselves in their own right and equally as valuable as they were before, rather than think of them as half a couple and somehow deficient for that reason.

I was taking a bin bag of Martin's clothes to one dear Friend for a charity she worked with, and she had prepared the most delicious tea with scones and sandwiches all spread on a lovely cloth. She listened to me and told me her family news, the ups and downs, all with a great deal of humour. Somehow she struck just the right note of 'life goes on, it's tough, but we can still enjoy it.' She is a widow too, so I knew she understood, and I could see what a survivor she is.

As the anniversary of Martin's death approached the memories intensified, and then, of course, it was Christmas again, and I was dreading it.

As it turned out some friends with children invited Margaret and me for a meal followed by fun and games. It was totally different and I thoroughly enjoyed myself.

*

Each season brings its own memories. I can remember the emptiness of the spring with Martin's large vegetable plot waiting to be brought to life by his special hoe and a generous mulching from the compost heap. I could almost hear the familiar sounds. It seemed a blank wasteland and I imagined a sense of accusation coming from it because of my lack of knowledge and energy to do the necessary work.

Spring and summer are times of renewed hope and enjoyment of life for human beings, and I found my sadness contrasted strongly with the general cheerfulness around me. Also people were out and about more and there was less possibility of hiding away.

The messages from Martin about not keeping his things, and living life for myself were mostly helpful, but a perverse part of me felt I was being urged forward to a future as a single person when I was still looking longingly back at our life together.

But the effect overall was bracing! By the end of the summer the vegetable garden had been drastically reduced in size and a smaller, more manageable plot had produced runner beans, courgettes and marrows. I had never grown vegetables before, and I enjoyed it. I even had enough to give away!

*

I often woke feeling a bit depressed and not wanting to face the day, especially on dark, rainy mornings. I was still listening regularly to Paul's tape, but I needed something more. The idea came to me to say 'Every day is a gift!' This suddenly seemed to put a new light on things, and I saw that the hours ahead could be an opportunity to enjoy myself, to help other people, and to try and achieve something worthwhile.

On January 21st 2005, thirteen months after his death, I wrote in my diary:

So, into the new year with my dearest one nearby and yet also in another place. I think I really have adapted well. 'Every day is a gift', and I must be grateful. But it's also just an interval, part of an intermission until we are together again, and in a sense not real.

*

The pain of my bereavement is now behind me. If I hadn't written down the strange and intense feelings I had at the time I probably wouldn't remember them clearly. But I recently spoke to a friend whose husband died three months ago, and who is going through the worst stages *now*. Listening to her, two things came back forcefully to me.

You think that no-one has ever felt as bad as you feel now,

and you *may* think at times that you are going out of your mind. In a CRUSE leaflet the emotions we may pass through in the acute stages of bereavement are listed as follows: numbness, agitation, anger, guilt, relief, sadness, and periods of time where we just sit or lie and do nothing. Sometimes strong emotions come in quick succession and can seem completely overwhelming; that is what is so frightening and so exhausting. All I can say is that this stage will pass. Try to take a day at a time. Even an hour at a time. Hold on. Ask for help.

Part II

For to one is given by the Spirit the word of wisdom; to another the word of knowledge by the same Spirit;

To another faith by the same Spirit; to another the gifts of healing by the same Spirit;

To another the working of miracles; to another prophecy; to another discerning of spirits; to another divers kinds of tongues; to another the interpretation of tongues:

But all these worketh that one and the selfsame Spirit, dividing to every man severally as he will.

For as the body is one, and hath many members, and all the members of that one body, being many, are one body: so also is Christ.

I Corinthians, chapter XII, verses 8-12.

Chapter 12

Mediumship, communication and the problems

Modern Spiritualism is said to have started at Hydesville, in New York State, on March 31, 1848. But its phenomena were noted in previous decades and in other lands... A hundred years previously, around 1750, Franz Mesmer, a German working in Vienna and Paris took interest in an old belief that magnetised rods had healing properties. He developed a technique, using these rods and verbal persuasion which proved to be quite successful and popular. An offshoot of this was that in some people it induced trance conditions during which many different types of phenomenon manifested.
(Jean Bassett. *100 Years of Spiritualism*.)

It seems that at the midpoint of the nineteenth century, those in the next world made an enormous effort to begin communicating with those on Earth, while those on Earth began to respond to them in a way they had not before. Primitive peoples have always retained the knowledge of trance states but this had largely become lost to the more 'civilised' nations.

Spiritualism as a movement began with a bang, or rather with rapping sounds loud enough to deprive a family of sleep and fill them with dread. Spiritualists still celebrate Hydesville Day, the day when Mrs Fox asked neighbours to come and witness the rapping sounds which could break out in her house at any time when her daughters, Margaret and Kate, aged fourteen and eleven, were present. The Fox family, farmers and practising Methodists, were seriously troubled by the strange events taking place in their house, in the little hamlet of Hydesville. The house had a reputation for strange noises which had driven away the previous tenants, a family called Weakman, but had not previously bothered the Fox family.

The parents prayed for the phenomena to cease but the rappings continued so powerfully that they could not be ignored. The communicator claimed to be Charles B. Rosma, a pedlar, and he was able to tell his story through a series of raps loud enough to make the walls of the house shake. Using a code devised by the girls, he told them that he had been brutally murdered for the money he was carrying, and buried in the cellar of the house.

Some 'experts' said the raps were produced by the girls manipulating their joints; however, the sounds were much too loud for this to be the case, and they continued when the girls were taken to the home of a neighbour to rest. The excavation carried out in the cellar at the time had to be abandoned when water was found under the floor, but in the summer the digging resumed and did indeed reveal some traces of human remains. At a depth of five feet a plank was found, and further digging disclosed charcoal and quicklime and finally human hair and bones which were pronounced by medical testimony to belong to a human skeleton. However, it was not until fifty years later, that the body of a murdered man and a pedlar's box were discovered under one of the walls of the cellar.

There were two reasons why the events at Hydesville were so significant. Kate, the younger sister, made a breakthrough. She snapped her fingers a number of times and asked the spirit to repeat the number back to her. The spirit did so. Next she mimed snapping her fingers, while making no sound, and the spirit again gave her the correct number in raps. So, the spirit could see as well as hear! This was apparently the first time communication with a spirit had been attempted.

The second reason for the significance of these events was that those who witnessed them rapidly formed themselves into a committee of investigation which took statements from the people most closely involved. *A Report of the Mysterious Noises heard in the house of Mr. John D. Fox,* was published and caused a sensation.

The adults, notably the mother, soon began to develop more sophisticated methods of communication with the spirit, and asked for answers to intimate questions. Mrs Fox, for instance, asked how many children she had:

I asked the noise to rap my different children's ages, successively. Instantly, each one of my children's ages were given correctly, pausing between them sufficiently long to individualize them until the seventh, at which a longer pause was made, and then three more emphatic raps were given, corresponding to the age of the little one that died, which was my youngest child.

I then asked: "Is this a human being that answers my questions so correctly?" There was a rap. I asked: "Is it a spirit? If it is make two raps." Two sounds were given as soon as the request was made. I then said: "if it is an injured spirit, make two raps," which were instantly made causing the house to tremble.

(From Mrs. Fox's deposition made a few days after the occurrence. Arthur Conan Doyle. *The History of Spiritualism.)*

The neighbours were called in, and their fascination with what was going on was so great that they continued to come in large numbers for several days until the exhausted family could hardly carry on with normal life. In fact, this was the end of normal life for Margaret and Kate. From then on the rapidly developing Spiritualist movement took over their lives. They were celebrities.

On the next Saturday the house was filled to overflowing. There were no sounds heard during the day, but they commenced again in the evening. It was said that there were over one hundred persons present at the time. (Ibid)

Margaret and Kate were not in the house, they had gone separately to the homes of two of their married siblings. The rapping at the Fox's home continued without their presence, and it also continued wherever the sisters happened to be. It was not long before rappings occurred in the presence of others, and as the movement spread there were other phenomena reported.

Leah, another sister, 19 years senior to Margaret, rejoined the Fox household on the break up of her marriage. She also exhibited mediumistic powers, which were said to run in the family. The girls had a grandmother and an aunt who possessed these gifts.

*

Charles Rosma's existence was never proved, despite the fact that he said he had a wife and five children, and there was enormous publicity at the time. But the story of a pedlar staying in the house was corroborated by a servant girl.

We have to turn to the deposition of Lucretia Pulver, who served as help during the tenancy of Mr and Mrs Bell, who occupied the house four years before. She describes how a pedlar came to the house and how he stayed the night there with his wares. Her employers told her that she might go home that night.

"I wanted to buy some things off the pedlar but had no money with me, and he said he would call at our house next morning and sell them to me. I never saw him after this. About three days after they sent for me to come back. I accordingly came back...

"One evening about a week after this, Mrs Bell sent me down to the cellar to shut the outer door. In going across the cellar I fell down near the centre of it. It appeared to be uneven and loose in that part. After I got upstairs, Mrs Bell asked me what I had screamed for and I told her. She laughed at me for being frightened, and said it was only the rats at work in the ground. A few days after this, Mr Bell carried a lot of dirt into the cellar just at night and was at work there some time. Mrs Bell told me that he was filling up the rat holes." (Ibid)

John Bell always protested that he was innocent of any crime and no charges were ever brought against him. He produced 44 character witnesses.

Charles Rosma now seemed to pass out of the picture, and other spirits with a greater mission took over.

In one of the communications the Fox sisters were assured that 'their manifestations would not be confined to them but would go all over the world.' This prophecy was soon in a fair way to be fulfilled, for these new powers and further developments of them, which included the discerning and hearing of spirits and the movements of objects without contact, appeared in many circles which were independent of the Fox family. (Ibid)

Hydesville became the centre from which the development of psychic powers spread in a way which was new and startling. Hundreds, perhaps thousands, of people began experimenting with this form of communication, many regarding the whole thing as entertainment, and with scant respect for the spirits.

The whole course of the movement had now widened and taken on a more important turn. It was no longer a murdered man calling for justice. The pedlar seemed to be used as a pioneer, and now that he had found the opening and method, a myriad of Intelligences were swarming at his back. Isaac Post had instituted the method of spelling by raps, and messages were pouring through. According to these the whole system had been devised by a band of thinkers and inventors on the spirit plane, foremost among them was Benjamin Franklin, whose eager mind and electrical knowledge in Earth life might well qualify him for such a venture. (Ibid)

Spiritualist churches were set up by those who saw the phenomena as central to a new religion; and those who wished to investigate scientifically began to do so individually and as members of societies for psychical research. At this time, when interest in the subject was at its height, a sort of craze for spiritual communication swept through the USA and Europe.

It seems that Quakers were present as witnesses to the early events in the USA. Isaac Post, mentioned in the quotation above, was a Quaker, and the records show that he went on to develop mediumistic gifts himself and, indeed, wrote a book called: *Voices from the Spirit World: being communications from many spirits.*

Another Quaker enters the story when the Fox sisters' powers were being investigated by a large gathering at a public hall in the town of Rochester, about twenty miles from Hydesville. Frustration at their inability to discredit the phenomena was turning some elements of the crowd hostile.

...Mr Willetts, a gallant Quaker, was compelled at the fourth public meeting to declare that the mob of ruffians who designed

to lynch the girls should do so, if they attempted it, over his dead body. There was a disgraceful riot, the young women were smuggled out of a back door, and reason and justice were for the moment clouded over by force and folly. Then, as now, the minds of the average men of the world were so crammed with the things that do not matter that they had no space for the things that do matter.

(Arthur Conan Doyle. *The History of Spiritualism*.)

At a sitting in New York in 1850, the following were listed as gathered round the table.

...the Reverend Dr Griswold, Fenimore Cooper the novelist, Bancroft the historian, Rev. Dr Hawks, Dr J.W. Francis, Dr Marcy, Willis the Quaker poet, Bryant the poet, Bigelow of the Evening Post and General Lyman. All these were satisfied as to the facts, and the account winds up: 'The manners and bearing of the ladies (i.e. the three Fox sisters) are such... as to create a prepossession in their favour.' (Ibid)

*

Britain had, largely, ignored the phenomena of psychic manifestation. One or two mediums were working in public. Georgiana Eagle demonstrated in front of Queen Victoria at Osborne House in 1846. But even this did not at the time excite great attention although later her work and investigations did. However, when in 1852 Mrs Hayden travelled from America to be introduced in England by Mr Stone, a mesmerist of note, much publicity was generated. Even more attention was given when she was joined in London by Miss Jay and Mrs Roberts.

(Jean Bassett. *100 Years of National Spiritualism*.)

In the USA and Europe, eminent men thoroughly tested the most gifted mediums of their day. In the UK, William Crookes,

Oliver Lodge, Arthur Conan Doyle and Alfred Russel Wallace were amongst them. In 1874 Wallace published *On Miracles and Modern Spiritualism,* and Crookes published *Researches in the Phenomena of Spiritualism.*

Everyone who experimented with an open mind could not help but find in favour of the belief that personalities who had survived death *were* communicating. In some cases this was very damaging to the careers of the investigators, because opposition from powerful people in the Church and the scientific world, who did not want the current world view shaken, was formidable.

Experimenting with physical phenomena where material objects are moved at a distance from the medium without contact produced more conclusive results than was possible with mental phenomena where telepathy, subconscious recall or sheer trickery were more difficult to eliminate.

Those who did not wish to be convinced stayed well away from the investigations and fastened onto any rumour of fraud, however unsubstantiated. Critics poured scorn on the positive findings from a safe distance, often putting forward ludicrous explanations in order to try and discredit what was taking place. After years of painstaking research, with D.D. Hume, Florence Cook and other mediums, William Crookes, a well-respected scientist and a member of the Royal Society, asked, (as many who followed him were also to ask):

"Will not my critics give me credit for the possession of some amount of common sense?" He also asked reasonably why they could not "imagine that obvious precautions, which occur to them as soon as they sit down to pick holes in my experiments, are not unlikely to have also occurred to me in the course of prolonged and patient investigations."

(David Fontana. *Is There an Afterlife?)*

For the sake of his career Crookes was forced to withdraw from research into what he had named 'the psychic force', and concentrate on more 'respectable' scientific work. However, in 1917, just two years before his death, he said:

"I have never had any occasion to change my mind on the subject. I am perfectly satisfied with what I have said in earlier days. It is quite true that a connection has been set up between this world and the next."
(Arthur Conan Doyle. *The History of Spiritualism.*)

Sadly, the detractors have been largely successful, and today Victorian Spiritualism is usually thought of as bizarre and ludicrous fakery. Undoubtedly, in some cases there was trickery taking place, but there was also genuine mediumship of a good calibre, which was carefully examined and evaluated by highly regarded and scrupulous investigators. The records they left are eloquent testimony.

The Fox sisters continued to demonstrate powerful mediumship throughout their lives, and passed triumphantly through countless such investigations. Their story is sad and controversial in many ways. So much needed to be understood about the proper exercise of these new powers, and how mediums and mediumship should be treated. The atmosphere surrounding them was always super-charged, with admiration and devotion from their supporters, and hostility from many in the Church, the scientific world and the press. It is a fascinating story, but so is the whole history of Spiritualism, which is beyond the scope of this book.

The question has often been asked, "What was the purpose of so strange a movement at this particular time, granting that it is all that it claims to be?" Governor Tallmadge, a United States senator of repute, was one of the early converts to the new cult, and he has left it upon record that he asked this question upon two separate occasions in two different years from different mediums. The answer in each case was almost identical. The first said: "It is to draw mankind together in harmony and to convince sceptics of the immortality of the soul." The second said: "To unite mankind and to convince sceptical minds of the immortality of the soul."

(Arthur Conan Doyle. *History of Spiritualism.*)

*

There is a wide variety of paranormal gifts, referred to by St. Paul as 'gifts of the Spirit'. They often arise spontaneously in childhood and, in our materialistic society, psychic children are often misunderstood and can become bewildered and withdrawn. They need special care and understanding and it may be necessary to seek help from outside the family.

Psychic ability is a gift as is music, painting or literary prowess. The main difference, of course, is that unlike these gifts it declares itself to the owner without any conscious effort. The psychic has the ability to raise his or her vibrations to a much faster frequency, affording access to sights and sounds beyond the physical level.

Mysticism, and indeed all personal spiritual experience, is the prerogative of all. This is the positive recognition of a separate spiritual identity and is only limited by physical inability to acknowledge and use it.

(Ivy Northage. *Mediumship Made Simple*)

The following description of an early psychic experience is from *Inevitable Journey*, the autobiography of a well-known medium, Donald Galloway. It is sadly typical of the experience of many children who possess the gift. Donald was six years old at the time and attending his grandmother's funeral. The underlining is added to emphasise the point I am making.

As the family stood with bowed heads around the graveside, the youngest boy found himself gazing up at the figure of his grandmother, standing alongside the Minister and looking at him with that well-known expression of hers! Consequently he was at a loss to understand why everybody gazed steadily down into the great six-foot-deep hole, totally ignoring the old lady whom they were supposed to be honouring with their presences, standing 'large as life' alongside the Minister! So riveted was the boy's attention at this unusual spectacle that he had to be nudged as a reminder to drop the lilies into the grave, this being done quite absentmindedly, the flowers falling in the mud down the side of the coffin. Reprimanded later for his carelessness, the boy found it useless trying to explain his regrets, so realised that it would be even more useless trying to gain understanding of the rather strange situation, <u>which must thereafter remain his secret</u>.

Psychic children may either be recognised and helped to develop the gift, may struggle against parental opposition but later in life find an accepting environment in which to develop, or may manage to suppress the gift altogether. Does such suppression lead to later illness or some other expression of disharmony within the personality? Whatever the circumstances of the psychically gifted person in our society, life and development is unlikely to be easy.

Psychic experience frequently begins early in life but it can, however, occur or resurface at any time in later life, and this can often cause great anxiety. If psychic experience begins to manifest in your own life take comfort from the fact that you are surrounded by love, and can at all times remain in control of the gift and of the extent to which it may manifest. Only *you* are in control, and only *you* can decide if you wish to go further along this path.

A one-off paranormal experience, such as sometimes occurs after the death of a loved one, does not necessarily mean that your own psychic or mediumistic powers are developing. It may simply mean that the links of love between yourself and the person who has passed on are so strong that he or she wishes, and is able, however briefly, to communicate their continuing existence.

Seek guidance inwardly through prayer or meditation on anything you don't understand, and perhaps ask for advice from someone with experience in these matters.

*

Betty Shine, a healer and psychic, wrote a series of books on the theme of developing what she called 'mind energy', in which she also tried to demystify the possession of paranormal gifts.

Practically all professional mediums and healers are down-to-earth practical people who do not consider themselves to be special. They use their talents every day and accept them as normal rather than paranormal. Just as with any gift – whether it's music, carpentry or surgery – the more the gift is used, the more adept one becomes.

And:-

... I think it is sad that the media so often seem to sensationalise mediumship, clairvoyance and healing. All these are perfectly natural gifts and good mediums do not go about with beads about their heads and wearing flowing gowns. Most of them are busy as well as very positive people whose role as they see it is to bring consolation to those who have lost family

and friends and whose religion, they feel, for whatever reasons, has let them down. (Betty Shine. *Mind to Mind.*)

In the foreword to *Mind to Mind*, Michael Bentine writes:

My close friend, Betty Shine, has an appropriate surname. Good humour, bubbling energy and down-to-earth honesty seem to radiate from her warm and attractive personality, making her any child's idea of the perfect aunty.

*

It is not easy to find a book which describes the process of mediumship in a way which is understandable by people who have no such gift themselves, or have never encountered it in another.

In 1999, I tried to throw some light on this misunderstood and divisive subject with my booklet *Continuing Life – the evidence for survival through mediumship*, which many readers say they found helpful.

Part of the difficulty arises from the terminology used and the fact that key words such as 'psychic' and 'medium' are often not fully understood, and may be used interchangeably. There is an important difference however, as David Fontana explains:

Mediumship has been defined in a number of different ways, but basically it is the alleged ability to receive communications from people who have died. There is an important distinction between mediums and psychics not always appreciated by those writing about the subject. While mediums claim to be in touch with the spirit world, psychics are confined to information from this world, which they gather telepathically, clairvoyantly, or precognitively. Many mediums take the view that all those with mediumistic gifts are also psychic, but insist it is possible to

have psychic gifts without being mediumistic.
*(*David Fontana. *Is There an Afterlife:*
A Comprehensive Overview of the Evidence.)

A 'medium', as the word suggests, is someone who is definitely setting out to link another person (the sitter) with a spiritual being (the communicator), who wishes to make contact and is usually closely associated with the sitter through ties of love and affection. Another word for medium which has come into use more recently is 'sensitive'. The word 'paranormal' may be used to cover both psychic and mediumistic experience.

Whilst on the subject of terminology I have chosen to use 'spiritual being' to describe an entity who is not operating through a physical body. In fact, we are all spiritual beings, of course, so this is not strictly accurate, but the alternative is to use terms such as 'discarnate entity' or 'those in the higher dimensions' which I find less acceptable.

And how to describe the worlds, levels, planes, dimensions beyond, above, and interpenetrating this Earth? I have chosen 'spiritual worlds' – again not wholly accurate but perhaps simpler and more in line with an attempt to de-mystify the subject as far as possible. I hope so.

*

There is a great difference between possessing psychic gifts and being a professional medium. A medium is someone with a significant gift who has dedicated his or her life to working to help link spiritual beings with those in Earthly life. Once this dedication has been made, wise beings in this dimension begin to work with the trainee.

Professional mediums have usually undergone a long period

of training, both inwardly with their own guides, and outwardly in some recognised form. Ivy Northage, who was a highly-respected teaching medium at the College of Psychic Studies, wrote several books on the subject. She had a Chinese guide, Chan, and mediums frequently *do* have ancient Chinese sages or North American Indians as guides - a further opportunity for derisory comments from the sceptics. As I understand it, however, the real reason is that these cultural groups (through the practice of Taoism and Shamanism respectively) place an emphasis on deep-seated spiritual harmony between Heaven and Earth which enables them, after death, to lower their vibrations sufficiently to work with mediums; a facility which other advanced spiritual beings find more difficult to achieve.

In the following extract Ivy Northage writes of her development:

... under Chan's gentle directive I learned slowly to recognise the needs of my nervous system and to adapt to the faster vibrations of the invisible planes. Throughout these formative years of training, Chan went to enormous lengths to establish my confidence in him. We had, by this time, built a mental association which enabled me to take his instructions directly in my mind rather than wait for my husband to repeat what I had said while in trance. The mental contact made it even more important to receive confirmation from outside. How could I tell it was not my own mind? Again, in this he never failed me and I learned to recognise and trust this form of communication with him. Once I had developed this mental contact I found it quite different from my own mind's activity. Chan and I still employ this person-to-person communication when I require special instruction on any aspect of our work together.

Spirit guides play an important part in the development and service of mediumship, and it is necessary to understand their function. I am often asked 'Does everyone have guides?' The answer is 'No'. We all have spiritual companions known as guardians from whom, no doubt, the term 'guardian angel' originated, but these should not be confused with guides.

The guides have attached themselves to the medium for the sole purpose of using their psychic gifts on behalf of humanity.
(Ivy Northage. *Mediumship Made Simple*)

Not everyone would agree with Ivy Northage that it is only mediums who have 'guides', another term which is often used quite loosely to describe the spiritual beings who offer their help and support to those in Earthly life, whether gifted mediumistically, or not.

Paul Lambillion says that whenever a group meets for spiritual purposes he sees more spiritual beings than Earthly people present in the room, and we are told repeatedly that those in the spiritual worlds are concerned for those of us experiencing physical life, and are interested in every attempt we make to contact them or understand more about the world in which they live. They are well aware of the problems that face us on many fronts and are willing to help us. But, of course, we have free will. We may ask for their help or we may choose to go it alone.

*

A professional medium spends most of his or her working life in one-to-one sessions, 'sittings', or 'readings', in which she (or he) attempts to establish a connection, on behalf of the client or sitter with their loved ones who have passed on.

All mediums first put themselves into the safe hands of their guides and helpers, and most will begin, inwardly, with the important ritual of asking for protection. The danger for people who experiment with communication for amusement or for wrong purposes is that they will be unprotected, and may open themselves to unwanted contacts with spiritual beings who are not very evolved, and are not coming with good intentions. Like, however, tends to attract like in the next world as in this, and our own spiritual helpers, though we may not have made contact with them consciously, are on hand to assist us. (I was recently asked if Quakers protect themselves when sitting in Meeting? An interesting thought.)

*

We know it is wrong to discriminate against anyone on grounds of age, sex, race, class, etc., and yet perhaps without realising it, do we not discriminate against those with paranormal gifts? We may give them a wide berth, feeling they are 'not for us', possibly unreliable, deceptive, even fraudulent. And in some cases we may be right, but there are many people working hard and with integrity to use their gifts for the benefit of others.

Madame Arcarti has a lot to answer for! Noel Coward's ever-popular play, *Blithe Spirit*, mocks Spiritualism with such brilliance that for years audiences have laughed at the misrepresentations of the phenomena portrayed and gone home with the comfortable feeling that the whole thing is a big hoax. And so, what many would like to believe has been reinforced, and many other plays, books and films have continued to spread misinformation.

It is an unfortunate truth that paranormal phenomena *are* easily mocked when reported second- or third-hand. However, a good medium on a good day can give such incontrovertible evidence of contact with loved ones that within a few minutes all scepticism falls away. This can only be truly appreciated through firsthand experience.

Donald Galloway describes the difficulties:

Every medium knows the great joy of those rare occasions when they can attain such a complete, free flow with one good communicator; which is like playing the part of host between two visitors – in this case, the physical sitter and the spirit friend. More often, however, a good line of communication – true spirit communication – does not hold for too long, other spirit people being anxious to get over just some small detail or other in order to feel a certain sense of achievement for themselves and to say to the sitter, in effect, 'I'm here, too.'

Acknowledging our existence within a complexity of inter-mental fields of many diverse energies and wavelengths, we realise why spirit friends also have much difficulty in penetrating the many layers of radiational activity in order to attain that perfect blending and delicate balance between individual minds – discarnate and incarnate – which alone makes for true communication.

(Donald Galloway. *Inevitable Journey.*)

And again:-

The style of any medium's presentation can change with each and every demonstration, public and private, according to the personal vibrations, mental, emotional and health states of the recipient of their work and indeed, the communicative vibrations of the many different spirit personalities endeavouring to make contact. The medium has to work hard in order to attain perfect balance of attunement for good spirit communication and, this being of a most intangible order, it is easy to see why it can be so easily thrown off-key. (Ibid)

When discussing mediums and communications most people who have not studied the subject seem to have little idea of the difficulties involved and little sympathy for mediums. Perhaps this is because they have never received any explanation.

The greatest difficulties are associated with differences in levels of consciousness. The communicator and medium need to attain the same level or vibrational rate in order for contact to take place: this means the communicator lowering their rate and the medium raising theirs.

*

The mediumistic gift expresses itself in a number of different ways, from purely mental mediumship at one end of the scale, with the medium consciously relaying messages, supposedly from the deceased, to physical mediumship at the other, in which the medium, usually in deep trance, is said to supply a form of subtle energy that is used by spirits to produce psychokinetic effects. (David Fontana. *Is There an Afterlife?)*

Physical mediumship is much less common than mental mediumship these days but a fascinating subject to explore. As it is less likely to be encountered, I have only mentioned it briefly in this discussion for reasons of space. If you would like to read in more detail on the subject I would recommend Robin Foy's book, "In Pursuit of Physical Mediumship", and Arthur Ellison's "The Reality of the Paranormal". Arthur Conan Doyle's "The History of Spiritualism" gives detailed descriptions of the phenomena experienced from 1848 to the 1920s. *(See reference section).*

Nowadays, most mediums use their gifts while they remain in full consciousness. Spiritual beings impress themselves on the medium by various means which we can understand as a heightened sense of seeing, hearing and sensation (actual physical sensation, or feeling as in emotion). These gifts are known respectively as clairvoyance, clairaudience and clairsentience.

Mediums possess them in various combinations and to varying degrees. The receptivity and sensitivity of the sitter is of great importance in this delicate operation. A wish to co-operate and a sympathetic presence are needed, and the sitter should be open-minded and not try to steer the session in a definite direction. A sceptical attitude is also damaging, which is the reason why many researchers fail to get good evidence! Powerful emotions like intense grief can also act as a block, so a bereaved person may be well advised to wait a little while before attempting communication.

When, as is commonly the case, the medium is conscious, sitters are usually requested to remain passive and answer little more than 'yes' or 'no'; certainly not to lead the medium who must attempt to relay accurate information without any prompting. In some cases communicators have difficulty and the link is tenuous. This is not the fault of the medium but it can make for uncertainty, and a strong communicator is to be hoped for. As will have been seen in my sessions with Paul, a quite robust (the word which always springs to my mind) conversation takes place with the medium in full consciousness. (Make a rule and it is sure to be broken.) However, the rule of not leading the medium should *always* apply. How else can we be confident that the communication is genuine? Sitters should never volunteer information, and if the medium starts fishing for it, then it may be time to start worrying and ask for your money back!

*

Communication may also take place with the medium in trance (or apparently unconscious), as Martin and I experienced in 1978, and I described in chapter 5. We were fortunate, because direct voice mediumship, as it is known, is rare and usually only happens in private groups (known as circles) where the medium is well protected.

Arthur Findlay, who donated Stansted Hall to be used as a Spiritualist College, writing of the Scottish direct voice medium, John C. Sloan, says:

I have had my ear close to his mouth on many occasions, when one or more voices were speaking at the same time, several yards away from the medium, and there was not a sound coming from it.

(Arthur Findlay, *The Rock of Truth.*)

One of the most famous direct voice mediums was Leslie Flint. Tape recordings made in the 1970s provide hours of the most fascinating and varied communications from the famous and eloquent and also the simple and humble. Many of these communicators were recognised and accepted as genuine by those who knew them in life, and long and regular conversations took place between the two worlds. It is interesting to observe how those who passed on some time ago had changed and modified the views they held while on Earth. I can only suggest that readers may like to listen to the tapes and judge for themselves. (*See the reference section.*)

*

Here is an extract from *Raymond Revised* – the book by Sir Oliver Lodge about his communication with his son, Raymond, who was killed in the First World War. The book first appeared in November 1916 and proved so popular it was reprinted twelve times before Lodge revised it in 1922. Sir Oliver, or O.J.L, as he calls himself, was Professor of Physics at Liverpool University and later Principal of Birmingham University.

A Mrs Kennedy (whose son Paul, another young soldier who was killed at about the same time as Raymond) was known to the Lodge family, through their mutual grief and interest in communication. Well into the sequence of contacts with the two young men, the following rather bizarre incident occurred. Sir Oliver Lodge writes:

On the morning of March 3rd, (1916) I had a sitting in Mrs Kennedy's house with a Mrs Clegg, a fairly elderly dame whose peculiarity is that she allows direct control by the communicator more readily than most mediums do.

Mrs. Kennedy has had Mrs. Clegg two or three times to her house, and Paul has learnt how to control her pretty easily, and is able to make very affectionate demonstrations and to talk through the organs of the medium, though in a rather jerky and broken way. She accordingly kindly arranged an anonymous sitting for me.

The sitting began with sudden clairvoyance, which was unexpected. It was a genuine though not a specially successful sitting, and it is worth reporting because of the reference to it which came afterwards through another medium on the evening of the same day...

After some description of the arrival of Mrs Clegg and the beginning of the sitting O.J.L continues:

Mrs Kennedy got up to darken the room slightly, and Mrs. Clegg ejaculated:-"Who is Raymond, Raymond, Raymond? He is standing close to me."

O.J.L then states, as proof that Mrs Clegg could not have known of him in this way, that his book about Raymond did not appear until 8 months later.

...After a time, with Mrs. Kennedy's help, the control seemed to get a little clearer, and the words "so glad; father; love to mother; so glad," frequently repeated in an indistinct and muffled tone of voice, were followed by "Love to all of them."

While Raymond was speaking, and at intervals, the medium kept flopping over to one side or the other, hanging on the arm of her chair with head down, or else dropping forward, or with head thrown back – assuming various limp and wounded attitudes...

It sounds from the medium's behaviour, and the fact that Paul, and to some extent Raymond, appeared able to speak *through* her, that she was in trance.

On the evening of this same 3rd March – i.e. later in the same day that I had sat with Mrs. Clegg – I went alone to Mrs. Leonard's house and had a rather remarkable sitting, at which full knowledge of the Clegg performance was shown. It is worthy of some careful attention.

Mrs. Leonard was the very well respected medium whom the Lodge family had visited for regular communications with Raymond. On this occasion O.J.L. was alone. It is a given that O.J.L., an experienced researcher, had not mentioned his sitting earlier in the day. Feda is Mrs. Leonard's guide.

Feda reported that Raymond had been at Paul's home and had tried to control an older medium, a new one to him. He wanted to speak through her, but he found it was difficult. Paul manages it all right, he says, but <u>he</u> finds it difficult. He says he started to get through, and then he didn't feel like himself. It's awfully strange when one tries to control anybody. He wanted to very badly; he almost had them. He means he nearly got through. Oh, he says, he's not giving it up; he's going to try again. What worries him is that he doesn't feel like himself. "You know, father, I might be anybody." He says "Do you believe that in that way, practice makes perfect?"

O.J.L. *" Yes, I'm sure it gets easier with practice."*

And so the dialogue continues. There is much more, but space does not permit... The point to emphasise is that there are also difficulties for our communicators to overcome as they try to contact us through different mediums: we need to bear this in mind. I sometimes feel people expect the clarity of a telephone conversation, but the whole process is far more complicated than that.

*

Some mediums are naturally more gifted than others. The more gifted do not usually need to advertise. Their time is fully booked for months in advance and so they are hard to find except by personal recommendation. There is also the question of wavelength, as mentioned above – perhaps quite literally. Just as we seem to have a natural affinity with some people and not with others, so we can find that a medium tunes in to us and our loved ones naturally or quite the reverse.

Mediums are also affected by their own state of health – tiredness, overwork, etc., their own preoccupations, and even the state of the weather. It should be remembered that providing a link with the spiritual worlds can be exhausting and draining to the medium. Mrs Leonard would only undertake two sittings in a day.

Mediums do have to be very mindful of their egos. As their powers are regarded as extraordinary - perhaps wonderful and highly enviable by some, while others will think them strange, even dangerous – it takes a spiritually developed and mature person to carry the gift successfully through life.

*

'Channelling' is a word which is used to describe communications which come from a spiritual being, either verbally or through the written word. It is rather as if an agreement is established between communicator and medium to make regular contact to give teaching, either through writing a book, or speaking to a group.

There is frequently a strong philosophical element to the communications and so they are of interest to the world at large. The teachings come from guides who have a mission to help humanity, and are usually given through those who already recognise that they have mediumistic ability and have perhaps been preparing themselves by praying and meditating and asking for such a contact to be made.

A notable example of written channelling took place after the death of F.W.H. Myers. Myers was a lecturer at Trinity College, Cambridge, and one of the founders of the Society for Psychical Research. Whilst on Earth he wrote many books on psychical research including the classic, *Human Personality and its Survival of Bodily Death.*

From the spiritual worlds he communicated *The Road to Immortality* through Geraldine Cummins. Those who knew him recognised the personality and style of Myers in the posthumous writings but, interestingly and unsurprisingly, Myers' views had been changed and modified somewhat by his new surroundings and his new knowledge, the book being communicated over the period 1924-31, over twenty years after his passing.

Geraldine Cummins was an exceptionally gifted 'automatist' (medium who has the gift of automatic writing), through whom about fifty personalities communicated. She was herself a writer of plays, of a novel, and of psychic works. Automatic writing is a paranormal gift which gives a particularly clear method of communication because the communicator seems to be able almost to dictate his or her words which are then written down at high speed by the medium in trance. Myers has a brilliant mind, and a deep almost obsessive interest in describing the next stages of life as minutely and lucidly as he can. As a life-long psychical researcher when on Earth, he knew the best method of getting his message through, and he found the best medium for his purposes. This is the process at work as described to Miss Cummins's friend and co-worker, Miss E.B.Gibbes:

The method employed by Miss Cummins in order to obtain the writings… is as follows. She sits at a table, covers her eyes with her left hand and concentrates on 'stillness'. She describes the result of such concentration in these words:

" … And soon I am in a condition of half-sleep, a kind of dream-state that yet, in its peculiar way, has more illumination than one's waking state. I have at times distinctly the sensation of a dreamer who has no conscious creative control over the ideas that are being formulated in words. I am a mere listener, and through my stillness and passivity I lend my aid to the stranger who is speaking. It is hard to put such a psychological condition into words. I have the consciousness that my brain is being used by a stranger all the time. It is just as if an endless telegram is being tapped out on it. The great speed of the writing suggests actual dictation, as though some already prepared essay were being read out to my brain. But something more than the faculty of amanuensis seems to be required. Whatever intelligence is operating, it may use my subconscious mind as an interpreter, may communicate in the language of thoughts or images and not of words… "

…It may be of interest to describe the manner in which the communications actually appeared on the paper. The writing of the name 'Frederic Myers' would be followed by 'good morning' or 'good evening, ladies'. A little friendly conversation would then take place and the request be made that the final sentences of the last essay be read aloud. The heading to the next chapter would then appear on the paper, a line being drawn firmly underneath it. The contents of each chapter in question quickly

followed.... If the 'psychic power' gave out, the writing would break off in the middle or at the end of a phrase. The actual writing is much larger than Miss Cummins's normal calligraphy and there is no division between the words. Generally speaking, the paragraphing and punctuation have to be inserted later.
(Geraldine Cummins. The Road to Immortality.*)*

Sitters often set stringent demands as regards the memories of the communicators. They frequently expect the discarnate mind to be exactly the same as the Earthly mind. Although it *is* very much the same, especially as regards the character of the person, it seems that details of the Earthly life have often become clouded or lost. Myers communicated this interesting piece on the difficulties of accessing Earthly memories when no longer in the physical body.

Memory out of the body is a different affair altogether. When we become discarnate beings we are far more detached from the early images for the reason that they are no longer bound to us by matter through the medium of the brain cells. The threads, you must realise, are broken by death. It does not mean that these images of all the impressions ever made on you are destroyed, they still exist, but we, when we choose can, under certain psychic conditions, draw those images we desire to us by making the effort of will that places us amongst them. We do not draw them to us as when we are alive, with labour and difficulty, we simply make the necessary effort which places us in the state that makes it possible for us to perceive the images we desire. Now, we are not in that state when we communicate through you. That is our difficulty. We are quite detached from these images, and unless the medium has the psychic power of absorbing the facts demanded from our memory – with our assistance, of course – we cannot provide you with the evidence you require. (Ibid)

*

Jane Sherwood, a Quaker, was lonely and desperate following the death of her husband, Andrew, in the First World War. She was warned by *"those who had experience, that there were certain dangers if one opened one's mind to influences from the spirit world."* In spite of this she tried to stretch her mind out into *"the great universe of real being searching for Andrew and... convinced that he was there."* She did not find Spiritualist literature helpful but eventually came to the ideas of Rudolf Steiner which were more acceptable to her.

A message from a friend through a Spiritualist medium indicated that Andrew was trying to make contact, and in further messages she was urged to try automatic writing. For two years she persevered with this without success and then one day the initials G.F.S. appeared on the paper and, as Jane relaxed her hand *"they made a name, a signature, G.F. Scott."* Even as she experienced the shock of success she felt too *"the impact of an emotion, a surprise and joy that matched my own."*

This was the introduction to a group of communicators in the spirit world, which included Andrew. Jane went on to write several books which are listed in the reference section. Between the wars she married again, less happily, and during World War Two she ran war-time schools in Saffron Walden and Llandrindod Wells. Then she settled in Wales and amongst other clerkships, became clerk of Mid-Wales Monthly Meeting. She died in 1990 at the age of 93, a much loved member of Chester Meeting. She was known for being extremely widely read and interested in discussing her beliefs and opinions. On one occasion she was turned down as a warden for a Quaker Meeting House because of her 'unorthodox views'.

*

There are many instances of mediums who channel a guide verbally (a form of direct voice mediumship). The medium is usually in a state of trance and relays the words of a guide, whom they have come to know and trust, to a group of people who may have been meeting over a period of many years for this purpose.

Ruth White has acted as a channel for Gildas for over 40 years, the contact beginning spontaneously in childhood. Ruth is a transpersonal psychotherapist and has a qualification in Counselling and Guidance. The following quotation is from her book *A Question of Guidance* in which she describes her perception of Gildas. She has written several other books. (*See the reference section.*)

'Gildas' is the name of the presence who is always near me, whom I identify as my discarnate guide. That is to say that I experience him as a separate personality, being, or entity, communicating from another plane of existence, and not from or part of a solely inner part of myself. I understand him (also by his own definition) to have been incarnate many times on the earth plane, but to be now in a discarnate state.

I am aware that his presence was with me from my earliest childhood. I did not know him then as 'Gildas' or as a 'guide'. Since he either appears wearing a white monkish robe, or in his glowing energy body, and since adults speak sometimes to children of 'guardian angels', if I thought about him, or questioned his presence at all, it was to assume he was an angel.

As well as awareness of this companion I saw the fairies and elementals in the garden. I saw the house fairies, and the fairies which come when there is laughter, dancing or live music. I saw the changing colours, and energy fields or auras around people and material objects.

It only dawned on me very gradually that the expanded world of which I was conscious was not only in some way 'different' but that it was questionable and unacceptable. The older I grew the more adults frowned upon my 'strange' perceptions, and comments. I became bewildered and withdrawn, and was considered a 'difficult' child.

...I now know him not as an angel, but as a discarnate guide and companion. I see him usually in his energy body full of pink, violet, white and gold colours of light, though in the early days of his reappearance I saw him more often as a monk in a white robe.

... Almost all that he has said about himself is that during his final incarnation he was a Benedictine monk in 14th century France, and that now he is part of a group from the 'other side', who are seeking to help individuals in incarnation on Earth, and also the planet of Earth itself. He, and presumably the group of which he speaks, are concerned with teaching, guidance and healing: they bring an input from their perspective which carries a message of urgency but also of hope.

(Ruth White. *A Question of Guidance.*)

There are two groups which meet regularly to hear Gildas's teachings, one in Pinner and the other in Oxford.

Ruth gives an interesting warning in her book, which I think is worth repeating:

Discarnate guidance is becoming a 'fashion', and even a 'cult' in these times and the pitfalls are many and often deep. The 'New Age' movement is too often used as a means by which individuals so sensitize themselves that they can no longer live comfortably in the world as we know it. Their energies become completely focused on making their own environment stress free with the result that they cannot be effective in outer living. I do not consider that this state should be the result of spiritual growth and training. Those who focus on their spiritual strengths can become more adequate in the outer world, and able to work there with the view to expressing spiritual values such as love and integrity to combat disillusionment, corruption and cold self-interested competition. (Ibid)

*

Other examples of spiritual teachers are White Eagle whose words were channelled by Grace Cooke, Helio Arcanophus (or H.A.) channelled by Tony Neate, and Eileen Caddy's channelling of a source she described as 'the voice of God'. All three of these series of channellings led to the setting up of organisations and centres which came into existence to live out and pass on their teachings to the world. They are, respectively, The White Eagle Lodge, with its temple at Liss in Hampshire, and branches throughout the world, Runnings Park in the Malvern Hills (which functioned effectively for many years but is now no longer in existence), and the Findhorn Foundation in Scotland.

*

In May of 2004, soon after Martin's death, I was whisked away by Margaret, my friend and neighbour, to attend a weekend course at Poulstone Court, which is a large rambling house in the Wye Valley. The course was an annual event and most of the people present had attended before. Some, many times. There were about forty of us and we spent most of the weekend sitting in a large room with wonderful views, and with the sound of sheep and lambs bleating in the fields around. There is a most beautiful garden where we did T'ai Chi before breakfast. The whole experience was very healing for me.

Pat Rodegast had come from the USA to visit Poulstone Court, and other places in the UK, in order to channel her guide Emmanuel. She sat quietly on the floor and it was almost as if Emmanuel was standing behind her. Sometimes she would speak as herself and then there would be a small pause and she would begin to speak as Emmanuel. When Emmanuel was speaking the voice was more confident and some of his comments and answers to questions were quite lengthy and complex but with a kind of compelling simplicity. They made sense and had the ring of truth about them.

In a book of Emmanuel's teachings (Pat Rodegast. *Teachings of Emmanuel*), are these words:

Don't speak ill of the dead.
That's nonsense.
There is no such thing as 'the dead'
in the first place, and the belief
that the dead must be protected
goes against reality.
In their lifted state of consciousness
they are better able to hear the truth.

Communication does not stop
at the doorway of death.
The wall between physical reality
and the spirit world is very thin,
as you can see by the fact
that I am standing here talking to you.

You in your element,
and the person who has died in his or her element,
can work on the same issues
and come to a deeper understanding
even though the illusion
says you are totally separated.

Your truth can propel the lifted one into growth.
Quite the opposite from what most people believe.
Even though it is comforting to recall
someone as you last knew them, it is guaranteed
that there has been a change for the positive.
There is something remarkably refreshing
and educating about dying.

I love this expression of the idea that communication goes on, and relationships continue to develop between those on Earth and those in the spiritual worlds.

I sat next to Pat at a mealtime and was interested to hear from her that people would often try to get a bit of private Emmanuel guidance from her by asking her to take a walk with them in the garden, or some such ploy. But Pat would only channel during the sessions and she is a completely different personality from Emmanuel so they would be disappointed. It's an easy mistake to make.

*

Paul Lambillion channels 'Heartstar' to a group which meets in a converted barn near Bury St. Edmunds. There are usually about twenty people present, most of whom are regular attenders. Interestingly 'Heartstar' is a label of convenience for, as with Gildas, a group of spiritual beings who link together to share their wisdom and experience with humanity. Like all guides they have had Earthly incarnations, but they have now reached a level of evolution where the individual personality is less important, and they are able to blend easily together and communicate as one.

After a few minutes conversation with the group Paul goes

into deep trance in which he remains for about an hour while Heartstar speaks through him. Watching him relax and hand over his body, it is possible to see the moment when the new entity arrives and begins to display different mannerisms. When Heartstar begins to speak, his voice and accent are also quite different from Paul's when speaking normally.

I think perhaps Paul feels a little left out on these occasions as when he re-enters his body at the end of the session, he is the only person in the room who has no idea what has been said. The sessions are always recorded, however, so he is able to find out later.

Here is part of an answer given by Heartstar to the question "Do you think life here has a pattern, do you believe certain events are bound to happen?"

Life has a pattern for each upon the earth. No two incarnated souls upon the planet Earth have been given the same objectives, and for each one of you the path you have to follow is different.

This is why when you compare your own particular circumstances with those of another, the exercise will be fruitless. For your path is for you and upon incarnation you are fulfilling pre-natal commitments which you have made with guidance from others, that you might work best to achieve both the refinement of your own soul and also be a support for the endeavours of those with whom and around whom you have incarnated.

And there is an optimum pattern for life with which you come to the Earth, and this pattern has quite specific objectives to its operation. There are certain parameters of expression in your life, and if you depart from them, then you will discover that your life can become more difficult and more painful. But if you work within the structure that you have been given, and if you seek always, as we have already said, to understand the

highest principles of life, looking for the opportunities, seeking to be full of optimism in the way you approach your life, then those circumstances which are difficult will begin to dissolve as you progress, growing in strength and in wisdom…
  (Paul Lambillion. *Communications from Heartstar.)*

*

Those in the spiritual worlds may impress on the human mind in many other ways: through musical composition, drawing and painting, for example, and through the 'dreaming' of scientific formulae . It may be argued that such impressions come from the subconscious mind of the individual and not from spiritual beings. The existence of these phenomena we should note in passing but cannot explore further in this book.

Do we regard healing as a psychic gift? This again is debatable. Friends have long been interested in healing and this very important subject is dealt with elsewhere in Quaker literature.

Chapter 13

"Nothing in life comes up to the immense joy of dying"

There was a time, when meadow, grove and stream,
The earth, and every common sight, to me did seem
Apparelled in celestial light...
William Wordsworth

As a young boy Paul Lambillion realised that he saw the world differently from the way other people saw it.

In adolescence I frequently observed light emanating from physical entities. People often shone for me, flowers radiated, rooms filled with colour, songs released bubbles of iridescence into the air and towns glowed with bands of fascinating energy. It was a colourful life!

When he sang in his school choir, which he much enjoyed, his 'sight' was enhanced and on one particular morning in the school hall, he had what might be described as a peak experience.

...The hymn 'From Glory to Glory', was one I especially loved, very powerful and stirring and still a favourite to this day. We sang it with verve and enthusiasm. The release of devotional energy mixed with boyish exuberance must have heightened my awareness. As I write these words my memory serves up

the delights of that special moment, I wish I could savour the experience again.

Around each boy and teacher, I saw two oval fields of coloured light, pulsing with gently flowing tones and hues and seeming to spin in opposite directions. One oval was slightly larger than the other and the two rotated at different speeds. Inside these remarkable forms the colours shimmered and radiated, changing and moving, first one way, then the next. The obvious underlying pattern of colour in each sphere was being modified as the singing progressed. It was a most spectacular and inspiring sight.

My jaw dropped when, from the crowns of several heads sparkling light strands of silver and deep violet darted upwards and outwards, like the most remarkable firework displays I had seen.

(Paul Lambillion. *Auras and Colours: A Guide to Working with Subtle Energies*.)

Like many psychic children, Paul learned not to share these wonderful experiences for fear of being thought either foolish or insane. He could not risk *"anyone trampling on my precious, dazzling world. It was too beautiful for that."*

*

The physical body is a wonderful vehicle for experiencing life on Earth; however, we all know its ultimate destination. And yet we are investigating the survival of the human personality beyond the point of death. It is natural to ask '*How* does it survive? In what form?' And this can be a huge stumbling block for the imagination... until we begin to consider the aura.

Everything is said to have an aura – the simplest plants, even rocks and stones. The complexity of the aura will relate to the complexity of the structure it surrounds. The human aura is an incredibly complex structure and I will do my best to give a simple impression of it, but as I cannot see it myself I am relying on the description of others, and of course, descriptions vary!

What I understand is that there is an inner or etheric aura (also known as the etheric body) which is shaped like the physical body. This is the blueprint of the physical body in finer form, coming into existence before it, bringing it into material form, and remaining with it until all signs of Earthly life have finally ceased. The etheric body interpenetrates our own, and exact replicas of each cell are said to exist. Changes in the physical body are preceded by changes in the etheric body. They can be seen and felt by clairvoyants, healers, those with the necessary gift. Some healers work on the aura and particularly the etheric body to treat problems which could later cause physical illness.

... All medical research could be improved if this etheric double was recognised and steps taken to observe its workings. Under such conditions it might be found possible to dispense with much of vivisectional research, which is often misleading, as certain tragic happenings in connection with the manufacture of drugs have made us aware.

(W.E.Butler. *How to Read the Aura.*)

The etheric aura receives energy (or prana or chi, if we are thinking in terms of Eastern religion and medicine) from the Sun, and other forms of energy from the Earth. It is from these energies that the etheric body derives its vitality.

Beyond the etheric body or inner aura, are the auras of emotion (sometimes known as the astral body), mind and spirit; the outer aura. This outer aura is composed of a series of intermingling sheaths. Whereas the distance the etheric body extends from the physical body can usually only be reckoned in inches, the combined emotional-mental radiation extends for several feet in the average person and in more highly developed people may exceed this. Again there is a quality of giving to, and receiving from, the environment. The aura is at all times registering the general emotional and mental quality and state of the person, being closely linked to sub-conscious thoughts and processes. The areas where energy enters the body at specific locations, which relate to major internal centres and organs, are known as the major chakras (eight in number – though Eastern philosophies teach that there are many more minor chakras) and are described as whirling vortices of energy. In diagrams and pictures in Eastern books they are often shown as having petals like a lotus. They are capable of opening or closing as the supply of energy is regulated. In disease states, the activity of the chakras often needs rebalancing within the whole system.

*

Many healers understand, 'read', and work on the aura, as it manifests in conditions of health and disease, in a way which is extremely detailed and specific. Many are able to *feel* it, some are able to *see* it.

Paul's gift for seeing auras has never left him, and nowadays he has learned to use it in a therapeutic way, to see where the strengths and weaknesses of a person might lie, and where disease may be manifesting at an early stage. As his website shows, he has developed a range of flower essences which he uses where necessary in addition to giving healing.

Martin developed as a healer in the early years of our marriage. He couldn't see the aura but he would hold his hands over a human being or animal and feel the strength and depth of the etheric body. He found the depth and resilience of this layer (the 'bounce') a quick test of general health. When a living creature is in poor health or near physical death this layer thins.

The size of the spiritual aura depends very much on the development of the person concerned. It can vary from a few feet to two hundred miles (as it was said to be in the case of the Buddha). St. Paul said: "In Him we live and move and have our being," as if the whole planet was held within the aura of a very great Being. The size of the aura is not an indicator of the use to which the person may put their power – psychic power can always be used for good or ill.

The aura is in a constant state of motion. Colours change and intermingle in swirls like mist as the condition of the person changes. Dark colours and solid-looking masses within the aura indicate areas of difficulty, which could be manifesting mentally, emotionally or physically. Soft pinks and golds with a free-flowing current of energy represent health and spiritual awareness. There may be shafts of energy, small or large, shooting out from the aura to influence the world around. Depending on colour and quality these could be darts of anger or beams of healing.

Perhaps there was a time when all humans could see the aura, and perhaps that time will come again, but in our culture it has become a very unusual gift, and thus, to some, a source of fear. Over the centuries those with unusual powers have been persecuted - killed, tortured, driven underground - and as these gifts often run in families, many gifted individuals who might have been born to future generations may have been lost to us.

The aura has often been shown in early Christian and Buddhist paintings, either as an area of light radiating out from the whole body, or concentrated more specifically around the head. Sometimes it appears as a disc behind the head. The North American Indian feathered headdress is also said to represent the aura. It is interesting to link Quaker ideas of the 'Inner Light' with this phenomenon.

It may be simplistic to say that it is the aura which contains and transmits our essence, or soul, when we pass to the spiritual worlds, but this is perhaps near enough to the truth. The aura is the part of our selves which is with us throughout life and continues on in some sense when the physical body dies.

*

The following is part of an article by Rosalind Smith based on the writings of the Quaker, Jane Sherwood. I think it is a beautiful account of the transition to the spiritual worlds. Interestingly, the 'mental body' is not mentioned in this description - an example of how different people perceive and describe the aura in different ways.

...we are more complex than just body and soul – "a more accurate analysis would prove that we have a purely physical body actuated by a body of sensation, working in co-operation with an emotional form, and these all interpenetrated by a spiritual mode of being."

(Jane Sherwood. *The Fourfold Vision.*)

These divisions can be more clearly understood as the physical body, easily visible as solid matter; the etheric body, which contains the blue-print (or the facsimile) of the physical; the astral body in which all emotion and feeling is present, the essence of the personality that has built up during the earth life; and, that which contains everything else, the spiritual body.

When a person dies, leaving behind permanently their physical body, there is an interlude in which they find themselves in their etheric body. And, for a while this experiences various states of consciousness, including sleep, until it too is shed leaving the astral body to wake fully on the astral plane. Interestingly the communicator says that it normally takes *three days for the etheric body to disengage from the physical, bringing to mind the biblical mention of 'on the third day he rose again'. Once on the astral plane one's thoughts begin to be much concerned with the life of Earth which has been left behind. The scenes and events now come back vividly in terms of their <u>feeling</u> content, and impressions of people, events and acts are now more real and comprehensive than when they were actually experienced. The difference now is that the feelings and reactions of other people are now included – "the effects of deeds on the lives of others must be experienced as intimately as though to do and to suffer the deed were one...where sorrow and wrong have been inflicted they must be felt." Not only is it justice, it is "redemptive suffering...a purely natural process, set going by the astral body itself which thus works to rid itself of impurity and disease." This brings to mind the biblical phrase 'As through a glass, darkly, but now face to face.'*

The astral body is that with which we experience feelings and emotions – often a very unruly part of ourselves when still on the Earth plane, and which requires a great deal of work and development. When we are no longer in the etheric body the astral body is the only visible part of us – and that only to others on that plane. Here we exist in a world of thought – we can 'think' ourselves from one place to another. We can think of another being with whom we would like to make contact, and, providing that they are on the same plane as ourselves, we can find them. However, if there is not an affinity between us then we cannot make this contact, or at least, not until one or the other of us 'catches up'. The great spiritual law of 'Like attracts Like' pertains here, and, as we develop and grow spiritually we will find ourselves progressing onto higher planes, with more highly evolved beings. And, although time is not measured in the same way as here on earth, it will still seem like ages for this process to be worked through .

The fourth aspect of our being is that of pure spirit, referred to throughout the communications as the ego-body (not to be confused with the Freudian concept of ego), and which, though totally invisible, can stand off from the other bodies and observe their doings objectively. It is the part which differentiates human beings from animals and which can say 'I feel happy' or 'I feel tired' – in other words it can be aware of itself. It is this ability which causes its feeling of separation from the environment and from other beings, its isolation.

The other work of the ego-principle is to infuse the whole of experience with the special value we call meaning...No clear thought or perception could emerge unless the ego was present to translate all this into terms of meaning. The meaning, or essence of a thing, is generated by the ego – otherwise it is just a meaningless object. Communication on the astral planes is by thought, not in actual words, but as meaning. Thus there is no language barrier, as meaning is the same to all; its other name is intuition.

(Rosalind Smith. *Article: The Work of Jane Sherwood.*)

*

If there is a life beyond death what will it be like? If we are to one day enter this new dimension what can we expect? What is it like for those who are already there? How are we to imagine them in their new surroundings?

What are the *fears* we have about communication with those in the spiritual worlds? That lying in wait for us on the other side are those with whom we had a difficult or painful relationship, perhaps even a relationship in which we were the victims of mental or physical abuse? If this is so, it is understandable given all the horror films, and frightening TV programmes and books which abound these days. Unfortunately, sensationalism sells.

The powerful emotions of horror and fear grab an audience. Stories of ordinary people in loving relationships are far less successful financially. These are the sad facts of modern life.

However, a study of the literature on spiritual communication quickly shows that we link with those we *love* and not with those we *fear*. Linking with those who have passed beyond death is bound up with the idea of a shared wavelength. We often use this expression in life about those we love – 'we seem to be on the same wavelength' – without perhaps giving very much thought to what it means. But it is a truth and through this shared wavelength we remain connected.

Here is a quotation from a book *Journey into Immortality* written by Aubrey Rose about his son, David, who died of cancer at the age of twenty-one. The messages came through the direct voice medium, Leslie Flint, and were recorded on tape cassettes:

I love you. I shall always be behind you every step of the way. There are people here you never mentioned. We are a much bigger, wider family. We are all one. I shall remain for a long time the individual as you remember me, although I shall be on a much different level in some respects.

People are being prepared. We are never alone. In the nights, when I didn't sleep I was never alone. Nothing can separate us. We are much bigger than we seem. I knew that I had a death warrant. It didn't worry me. I was worried about you. The things I might have done I can do here. Everything here is much more real than you will ever know.

We are like brothers and sisters, much more than that. We are not that far away as you might think. Time for us is not as it is for you. We are a family, a much bigger family than you can imagine. Some have been here for centuries. Never grieve for me. I love you.

David's father adds:

David's words flowed clearly, unhesitatingly, with such a sense of affection and attachment. I reproduce here only extracts. He was now with us here at home, not merely a sense of his presence, but his very words.

...As the sittings continued, I learned much about myself, my family, my past, occasionally future happenings, confirming the strange nature of time, space, communications, raising a host of questions, leading to a revaluation, not of values, but of many commonly-held assumptions. Time, we were told again and again, was meaningless, an illusion, certainly in their world of colour and spirit. The injunction not to 'call up the dead' was described as complete nonsense. No one could call up the dead. It is the so-called 'dead' who wished to communicate and talk with us, when conditions were right. And our conversations were so natural, so relaxed, so detailed, often so joyous and full of fun, that to think of them in terms of etherealised mystery was absurd.

(Aubrey Rose. *Journey into Immortality*)

The above extract is particularly important because it deals with a commonly held prejudice – that 'it is wrong to call up the dead'.

Perhaps we should consider another prejudice against spiritual communication and that is the notion that people get hooked on it and neglect their own lives in favour of huddling in a darkened séance room. Yes, some people do get trapped in this way, but there is the danger of addiction in many areas of life. The addictive personality is always liable to find something to latch onto and it could certainly be mediumistic messages. But addiction hasn't been my own experience and I haven't seen it in others. Some people do continue to stay in occasional contact through a medium over the years, as David's family did, and as I have with Martin, but for most people just knowing that a loved one has arrived safely is enough to comfort and satisfy both parties. There is much to do in both worlds and while we are busy doing it, or in the quiet of the night-time, we can talk to our loved ones in our hearts. They see us and hear us and they understand much more clearly than we do that the link remains unbroken.

Also while in the sleep state, it is said that our astral bodies may enter the astral plane and meet with our loved ones, although on waking – as in my case – we may not retain the memory.

We should also reflect on the devastation which the grief of separation can have on loved ones in the new life. We understand our own grief because we experience it, but do we consider theirs?

Sally, the daughter of novelist Rosamund Lehmann died of polio as a young married woman. Eventually, she established contact with her mother:

You must understand a piece of me is always near you. It is as though I am free and exploring other states and dimensions, but a piece of me is with you. I know how you are feeling and when you are sending your love.... I can send serenity, and I can send protection and...quietness when you need these things.... But for many people this is not the case at all. Either their families cease to think of them or they send such queer shut-in thoughts, full of grief and limitations. This causes great discomfort here, and we are in agony when some people hear the thoughts of their earth links.

(Rosamund Lehmann. *The Swan in the Evening.*)

*

Accounts of the experience of death abound and also accounts of 'dead' relatives and friends coming to greet those whose death is impending. Selecting quotations was extremely difficult as all the accounts are fascinating. First, I have included one which describes the time just before dying, and then two accounts of death as witnessed by those experiencing it.

My grandfather died shortly before his 95th birthday at our home where, at the time, we were bringing up our three young children. He had joined us for a large family Christmas party but contracted pleurisy from which, despite the best of care, he did not recover. He was a retired Welsh Congregational minister - still preaching by invitation in his final year - and a man of unwavering faith, joy and great wit and humour. On the last day of his life he insisted on being helped out of bed so that he could sit in a chair and smoke his pipe and, at that point, he said quite calmly, "Well, I'm off. I'm leaving you tonight" - and he did.

After getting back into bed he slipped into intermittent sleep or coma but did not speak again until late into the night. Then, quite suddenly, he lifted his head and turned it towards a side door leading to the bathroom, exclaiming loudly and with delight, with a radiant smile of recognition on his face, "Annie!" Whether in reality or imagination, he was undoubtedly seeing and greeting his late wife - calling her by her 'young' name for her rather than the customary 'Mama' which he had consistently used after the arrival of his children.

For those of us who witnessed it, it was an incredibly moving and inspiring moment and we were left convinced that, as is reported in so many 'near death' experiences, my grandmother (who had suffered from Alzheimer's disease for many years before her own death twenty years earlier and who had not been referred to at all during my grandfather's final illness) had somehow come to 'meet' him at the moment of his death in order to 'hold the hand of a stranger in Paradise' (to paraphrase the old song!) That experience proves nothing, of course, but it remains a treasured, powerful and encouraging memory for those of us who shared in it.

This account was written by Jill Inskip for *The Not Unfamiliar Country: Communication Beyond Death, An Anthology of Quaker Experience.*

Now, here is a description of the event of physical death communicated by a diplomat, Sir Alvary Gascoigne, to his sister, Lady Cynthia Sandys:

*Every part of me seemed to be switching off gently, and ...I suddenly found I was floating above my body .... Nothing in life comes up to the immense joy of dying, ... I told you that I had experienced a strange feeling of power that seemed to be drawing me out of my body during the last few days of my illness....I welcomed the inrush of new life and let go very willingly. That was why I did not linger... You must be ready to receive the power that draws you quite painlessly out of your body. It's the most beautiful and glorious thing. I see many are prolonging their life quite unnecessarily .... Life commands you; you agree and co-operate. (*Cynthia Sandys and Rosamund Lehmann. *The Awakening Letters.)*

The next extract is from Frances Banks who communicated through her friend, Helen Greaves. Frances Banks was a powerful personality, a Sister in the Anglican Community of the Resurrection in South Africa for 25 years and for much of that time Principal of the Teachers' Training College. For the last years of Frances's life, she and Helen worked together on psychical and spiritual research in preparation for writing a book. That book was never written but a month after her death in November 1965, Frances established contact with Helen and the resulting *Testimony of Light* is much-loved and much in demand. It is reprinted frequently by the Churches' Fellowship for Psychical and Spiritual Studies.

Martin and I heard Helen Greaves lecture to a large audience at the College of Psychic Studies soon after we were married and were impressed by her simplicity and the quiet integrity which radiated from her.

As soon as I was able to bring myself to a conscious state of mind, after my withdrawal from my worn-out body, I knew that I was the same in essence. True, I felt light, and there was a new sense of freedom that was bewildering. I was the same ... yet not the same! With a flash of realisation I decided that I must be stone deaf, for I could no longer hear any of the usual sounds of every-day life, the chatter and movement of human beings around me; the whistles of trains, the twittering of birds ... There were no noises in this new consciousness. One of my first recollections was 'I am conscious, the change has taken place ... But I cannot hear, neither can I see!' And for a space of time I seemed to lose my identity ... I recall endeavouring anxiously to pierce through this new state to recall memory. 'Who am I? What did I do?' It was a strange, almost eerie experience, for the name I had borne for over seventy years eluded me ... At length I recall telling myself to 'Give it all up and go to sleep' and, in a way, this is what I must have done. At least consciousness went from me. I remembered nothing more. How long this went on I have no possible way of knowing ... perhaps in earth time, for a very short space.

But when I next came back into consciousness I seemed to be pulling myself up out of a thin sea of silver ... Those are the only words I can use to describe the experience. And the first face I saw was the smiling face of my dear Mother in religion – Mother Florence. I was so overwhelmed I couldn't speak. ... From then

on I remember that I seemed to be in and out of consciousness... But now I found that I was lying in an open porch with a vista of blue and silver before me... This was beautiful beyond words and calming to my spirit. Trouble, anxiety and all sense of loss abated; a great feeling of peace enwrapped me.
(Helen Greaves. *Testimony of Light.*)

Paul Beard, President of the College of Psychic Studies from 1966 to 1982, researched mediumship over many years. His books *Survival of Death*; *Living On* and *Hidden Man* are excellent guides to understanding communication and the worlds we encounter after death, in which he takes great care to address all the questions which occur to the intelligent reader when this subject is considered. He was a deep thinker and a meticulous researcher who drew on a wealth of material to substantiate his arguments. He passed over in 2002, at the age of 95.

My particular task is to seek contributions from post-mortem minds of good calibre. If a report were to appear on an unannounced Arctic or tropical exploration we would examine it for internal coherence and then examine the reputation for truth and integrity of those who produced it. If people who on earth were of substance and integrity claim to send back after their death reports of what they have found, these are worthy of being read with special care. Those to whom the reports were addressed, and who express confidence in them, must expect to find their own integrity similarly scrutinised. This is perfectly fair. (Paul Beard. *Living On.*)

Paul Beard gives this example of the circumstances that may arise after a sudden death, such as in a wartime situation:

Those who are killed quite suddenly ... come over with the feelings and thoughts which they had just before, often it is those who still think they have to go on fighting and have to be calmed;

often they think they must have suddenly gone mad, because the scene has changed. This is not surprising if you can imagine in what a tremendous state of tension, almost like madness, the actual fighting is carried out. Then they often think ... they are now in a base hospital ...

We have to humour them at first and only gradually explain to them what the hospital means. Sometimes they are profoundly glad, those who have come to the limit of endurance, and rejoice to be free of the world of wars. Sometimes, with those who have very strong home ties, we have to let them realise as gradually and gently as possible; most are so weary in spirit that they worry very little, and are soon ready to settle down to their rest.

Others have foreseen that they must be killed, they have seen the shell or bomb about to explode, and have known that when it explodes they must go.

(Paul Beard. From 'Joe's Scripts' as quoted in *Living On*.)

Paul Beard goes on to describe other meetings with loved ones. Sometimes a degree of adaptation in dress and look by those who greet the newcomer is necessary to ensure that they are recognised. Here is a description of such a situation from Helen Salter, psychical researcher and medium, who was well prepared for such events. Her parents were Professor and Mrs Verrall who were founder members of the Society for Psychical Research, and her husband, W.H. Salter, was Hon. Secretary of the Society.

My parents, A.W. and Margaret, came from regions and appearances beyond my ken and adopted the old disguises. These are all in the litter of memory. They have appeared to me, as I remember them in the earlier years of my life. They brought with them my very old-fashioned home of long ago and its dear, comfortable ugliness, its books, its papers and its flowers, even the photographs that figured in numbers in Victorian sitting rooms, drawing rooms and studies. How I am enjoying its dear atmosphere! I was very tired and it has been so restful to me – imbued as it is with the fragrance of so many distant memories. Oh, it will change, I know. Later on – visitors, friends, the setting of another scene in my life.

(Cummins, Geraldine. *Swan on a Black Sea*. Quoted by Paul Beard, in *Living On*.)

Paul Beard explains:

It can clearly be seen ... that accounts given soon after death present a picture much more like life on earth than is really the case. This apparent physicality has been the basis of much scorn and misunderstanding by hostile critics. Nevertheless, true experience can be wrapped in illusory appearances. In some respects it is rather like a dream world. The dreams we take to a psychiatrist are not regarded literally, but they point to very important psychological factors in the dreamer.

Early discarnate life is not wholly dreamlike but partly resembles it; like dreams it contains rapidly changing imagery; unlike dreams this imagery sometimes becomes stable and anchored for considerable periods, like Helen Salter's home; again, unlike dreams, the imagery is not created wholly by the dreamer, but also others who help him. In common with important dreams, early discarnate experiences point to and express the mental and emotional situation with the newcomer; other persons, essentially free of the dream themselves, may yet choose to step in and share it for a while, in order to help the newcomer, although their true life lies elsewhere. This is clearly true of Helen Salter's parents. Most important, those who are confined within their after-death dream usually take what is around them to be completely objective. Once they begin to see that it is not so, then they are beginning to be ready to step out of it into a larger world. Helen Salter was exceptional in being aware of this from the first.

*(*Paul Beard, Living On.*)*

Following death there comes a stage of sleep. Harvey Humann writing in a helpful little book, *Death Without Fear*, says:

There seems to be more unanimity about a sleep stage following death than any of the other stages. The consensus is that the average person who dies a natural death sleeps between four and five days. The nature of that sleep varies with each individual, his or her age, the intensity of suffering prior to death and the spiritual evolvement of the individual. The sleep stage is a very necessary stage of conditioning before we enter the spirit world.

Those who have a deep-seated conviction that death is the absolute end have a very long sleep stage. Those, however, who expect to survive and have some knowledge of the next world, do not necessarily need a sleep period unless they have had a long illness.

... One discarnate source said the thing which impressed him most after a period of sleep was the intensified reality of everything. Everything was more brilliant, the trees, the flowers, the landscape. Again, there is repeated reference in these accounts to the fact that the degree of expanded consciousness immediately following death is in direct proportion to the degree of spiritual evolvement.

*(*Harvey Humann. Death Without Fear.*)*

*

In the early stages of life in the spiritual worlds we learn to move and communicate much more swiftly than we are able to on Earth, and also to develop the ability to change our surroundings to a certain extent by means of thought, as shown in the earlier quotation from Helen Salter. We return to Living On for two separate communications:

There are things ... of the same kind as you see on earth, only somehow different. They are real, but you have a sense that they are only temporary, that they just belong to that first waking stage.

Then you find, and it seems very curious and fascinating, that you can change those things by wishing them to change. You can only do it with quite small and unimportant things, but for instance – you can look at a pine needle on the ground where you are sitting and begin to think of it as a real needle, a steel needle, and then it is an ordinary sewing needle and you can pick it up.

You can't change big things, you can't change the whole scene around you. That is because it is not only your scene, it belongs to lots of other spirits too, but you can change any little thing when the change won't affect anybody else. Then you begin to realise that all the things around you are really thought forms, and that it is arranged like that so as to make the transition from material life to spirit life. You learn a great deal simply by finding out what you can change by changing your own thought about it, and what remains unaltered however you think about it.

That makes you understand how little belongs to you alone so that you can do exactly what you like with it individually and how much belongs to the whole concourse of spirits of which you are a part.

(Paul Beard. 'Joe's Scripts', *Living On.*)

And:

On earth a great deal of effort has to be expended in order to make an impact upon its material density, rather as the mountaineer can only slowly cut each step before him as he makes his way up the ice slopes. The traveller now has to learn how he can transform the ideoplastic and malleable material he now encounters. Whilst some continue to take it that the physical appearances they observe are much as of old, others are more alert and recognise readily that the 'matter' now surrounding them is different.

...Picture it for a moment: you live in surroundings that resemble those you knew on earth. You are, it is true, freed from money worries, freed from the need to earn your daily bread. Your etheric body is nourished by light which is not the light of the sun. It is possessed also of energy and life. It does not suffer pain, nor is it subjected to struggle of any kind. It is indeed as if you lived in a pond, and soon you weary of the limitations of that calm unruffled sheet of water. You yearn for struggle, effort, ecstasy; you long for wide horizons. The call of the road has come to you again. (Ibid)

The quotations above suggest that the world we inhabit in the early stages of life after death is similar in appearance to our Earthly world. We are still conscious of ourselves as having a body but our bodies and the 'matter' around us behave differently.

According to those who report back to us, the world to which we awaken after death is a world where justice prevails, liberally tempered by mercy. There is always help on hand from more advanced beings of great compassion, for those who seek it.

It would be wrong to tell only of a world of light and beauty and it would be untrue and unbelievable. We all have a sense, if we have a sense of it at all, that the next life must reflect a variety of states and conditions. If the soul is to evolve it must experience what it requires at each stage in its progress, and if we need to realise our soul has become trapped, then we shall do so, literally, in the spiritual worlds. The conditions we find ourselves in are of our own creation and if some find themselves in darkness and despair, longing to return to Earth because of the pull of their physical natures and their own selfish desires, this state is of their own making and progress is always within their power.

The teachings about Heaven, Purgatory and Hell therefore have a ring of truth about them as do the teachings that there is a Judgement to be undergone. The Judgement, however, is described as a process in which *we* are the judges of our own recent Earthly life and where *we* experience within our new minds and bodies the consequences of our actions as they were experienced by the people they affected while we were on Earth. Again, spiritual beings of great compassion care for us and guide us through the process which is taken at a pace of our own choosing and is entirely directed towards our soul's enlightenment.

I find the idea of judgement reassuring as well as a little challenging. 'It's not fair!' is a phrase small children learn early, as the world of their own needs and desires collides with that of the adults who care for them. And that phrase goes on being repeated throughout life. We have a strong sense of justice and yet, so often in this life, the powerful rather than the good seem to reap the rewards. Discovering from communicators that we are indeed called to account seems to restore the sense of justice deep within us and also indicates that the Universe is not at all a meaningless, purposeless place. Knowing that we shall be called to account means that we have an opportunity to prepare, perhaps make reparation for wrongs done, while still on Earth.

Here is an example from the communication of Frances Banks, the Anglican nun. Frances was well prepared to enter the spiritual worlds and her joy in her new state of being is a delight. A spiritually aware person, as well as being knowledgeable about the new conditions, she progresses very quickly and is soon helping others. Here she is writing about the 'Judgement'.

...the whole cycle of your life-term unfolds before you in a kaleidoscopic series of pictures. During this crisis one seems to be entirely alone. Yours is the judgement. You stand alone at your own bar of judgement. You make your own decisions. You take your own blame.... You are the accused, the judge and the jury.

This is where quite a few souls in this Rest Home have become immobilised. Their pictures are too searing in their exposures. So we try to help them along, but only when they have made the 'inner desire' to right their wrongs. Until that decision I do not know what happens to them, but I should think that they are 'prisoners of the self'.

Immediately they become ready to face themselves again they are guided to those beautiful and peaceful homes. Here, the Sisters devote their love and thought, their skill and experience to aiding the 'stumblers'.

The second stage of the recapitulation starts when the soul feels strong enough and calmed sufficiently to take the earth life, round by round (so to speak). Then the blueprints are brought into the mind again; only this time the start is made from the moment of the departure of the body. The mind works slowly, oh! so slowly, backwards through one's experiences. (I am not confessing where I have reached in this exercise!) But I will tell you that now you seem <u>no longer alone</u>.

'Someone' is beside you. Whether it is your own High Spirit or a Great Helper I have yet to discover. Only now, as you ponder, work out, go over, tabulate and judge what you did AND WHY AND WHAT WERE THE RESULTS (good or bad) you are gloriously aware of this great Being beside you, giving strength, peace, tranquillity and helping with constructive criticism. This is a wonderful experience, though harrowing at times. But very cleansing and bringing new hope.
(Helen Greaves. *Testimony of Light.*)

Do the communications received give similar information about the spiritual worlds or do they contradict one another?

By and large communicators seem to be experiencing similar conditions. Conan Doyle in *The History of Spiritualism* agrees:

It has been said that these narratives vary greatly and are contradictory. The author has not found them so. In a long course of reading in which he has perused many volumes of alleged posthumous experiences, and also a great number of scripts obtained privately in families and reserved from the public, he has been struck by the general agreement. Here and there one comes upon some story which bears self-deception written plainly across it, and occasionally there is a lapse into sensationalism, but in the main the descriptions are sober, reasonable, and agree in general type with each other, even when they differ in details.

*

Nowadays with the improvement in resuscitation techniques, more and more people are having near death experiences (NDEs), and much research is being carried out in this area. There are some striking resemblances between NDEs and the descriptions of the first stages of life in the spiritual worlds which come to us through mediums:

No two near-death experiences are identical and there are some profound cultural differences. And yet within a culture there are uncanny similarities between them, common elements which crop up over and over again regardless of the person's age, sex and even independent of their religious faith or lack of it. In a Western culture these are, first, overwhelming feelings of peace, joy or bliss and the complete absence of any feelings of pain the body may have been feeling. Often the person feels as though they leave their body and look down on it from some vantage point near the ceiling. They may enter darkness, usually a dark tunnel through which they travel towards a pinpoint of light which grows larger and brighter as they approach it. The light seems to act as a magnet, drawing the person in. At this point they may meet a 'Being of Light' – a religious figure if they themselves are religious, or simply a 'presence' which is felt to be God or God-like. At some point they may come to a barrier, which is sensed to be a point of no return, beyond which they cannot go. Dead friends or relatives are sometimes seen on the other side of the barrier; indicating to them that they must go back, that it isn't yet time for them to come; often some quintessentially English garden or landscape is glimpsed beyond the barrier. A few people experience a 'life review'. Sometimes this is experienced as a kind of Day of Judgement in which the person's past actions are reviewed, but there is very seldom a feeling that you are being judged by some other being. Much more often is the conviction that you are your own judge, reviewing your own past actions, but with an awareness of their consequences and the pain you may have caused to others. Finally there is a return to the body, rapidly 'snapping back' as though on the end of an elastic cord.

For most people the near-death experience is one of the most profound they will ever have, and is vividly remembered

throughout their lives.
(Peter and Elizabeth Fenwick, The Art of Dying (c) 2008. Reprinted with the permission of the publisher, The Continuum International Publishing Group.)

*

Children also have near-death experiences. Melvin Morse, a paediatrician and acknowledged leader in the field of near-death research in the US, has treated many terminally ill children who have had NDEs and seen the Light. In his book, *Closer to the Light: Learning from Children's Near-Death Experiences*, he writes about those who have had this special experience, whom he calls 'Children of the Light'.

As I dipped into books about the terminal illnesses and deaths of children I was amazed to read story after story about children who appeared wise beyond their years. As they neared their deaths they seemed able to slip easily from this world into the spiritual worlds and back again without fear, as though they were being prepared for their passing and were also learning how to help their parents prepare. I began to feel vaguely uneasy. The stories of these sage-like little beings were almost unbelievable, and then I re-read a book by Elisabeth Kübler-Ross, *Death is of Vital Importance*, which gave me a possible explanation.

Elisabeth Kübler-Ross, was a psychiatrist and a pioneer in Near Death Studies. She wrote and lectured on the stages of grief, palliative care and the importance of understanding and validating spiritual end of life experiences. Her understanding, based on long experience of working with terminally ill children, is that as their physical difficulties increase, making normal life and development impossible, they seem to gain an enhanced spiritual awareness almost by way of compensation.

*

This story was told to me some years ago by one of my sisters. In the early nineteen sixties she had a baby girl, Alison, who was born with spina bifida and hydrocephalus. She died at the age of three having never been able to walk. Years later one early morning as my sister lay between sleeping and waking she became aware of a lovely young woman sitting on the end of her bed. She knew that it was Alison who would then have been in her early twenties. She asked Alison to show her that she could walk and Alison stood up, walked across the room and then disappeared.

Children grow up in the spiritual worlds loved, cared for and guided as they would be in a happy family on Earth, and retaining a strong connection with their loved ones in the physical world who will one day join them. Just as Martin has been given the task of working with the mineral kingdom, other souls take on the task of caring for children in the spiritual worlds. Often, we are told, they are women who longed to have children whilst on Earth but were unable for some reason to do so.

Children have always been amongst those who communicate after death either through mediums or directly with their loved ones. Here is a story from Sylvia Barbanell's book, *When a Child Dies*.

When thirteen year old Norma Sinclair was struck by a motor lorry and killed, her parents were devastated by grief. Eventually they were put in touch with the Spiritualist movement and Mr. Sinclair arranged a private sitting with the famous medium Helen Hughes. He was a complete stranger to her, she only knew his name.

...she described a tall girl who was standing by his side.

Then to his astonishment she went on to say "Furthermore the girl has put her arms round your neck, claiming you with love. She tells me you are her Daddy." Mr Sinclair says that Norma was a tall girl for her age. She never addressed him as "Father", but always as "Daddy".

When Mrs Hughes continued, "she has a brother with her," the father's heart sank. Norma was an only child. "That is absolutely impossible," he answered. "I never had a son." But the medium insisted. "My guide tells me," she affirmed, that it is indeed your own son. You never knew him in life on earth, as your wife had a miscarriage years ago. In the spirit world, your son has been named John, after your uncle John who has also passed on." He had, until that moment quite forgotten that, 15 years previously, his wife had a miscarriage. The statement about his uncle was also accurate.

As you will read elsewhere, evidence of Survival has been furnished by many spirit individuals who never breathed on earth at all. Once the spark of life has been ignited, growth continued at whatever stage of earthly life the physical counterpart of the spirit body perished.

Sylvia Izzard told me of a similar experience in connection with a miscarriage, and I asked her to write it down.

In May 1963, during my first marriage, I had a miscarriage – this would have been my second child. It was a particularly unpleasant experience both emotionally and physically and I was never told what sex the baby was.

At a sitting I had at Stansted Hall over forty years later when I was happily married to my second husband, Jim, a surprise greeted me when the medium, a pleasant lady from Wales, said: "I have a baby here in the spirit world."

I confirmed that I had lost a baby, and she then went on to tell me that this baby, a boy, had now grown into a young man.

This seemed too much for my mind to absorb. I suddenly felt all the emotional pain I had experienced in 1963, yet, at the same time, I was overwhelmed with a feeling of warmth and happiness.

As I approach the later stages of my life I feel a sense of excitement in that I can look forward to meeting the son I never knew on Earth.

*

As I look through the various books I use for reference, I find that the question of reincarnation is one on which writers find it difficult to agree. It is also a subject which is of great interest and frequently asked about. I think that the answer may be that as a process it is much more complicated than we at first imagine. Here is an extract from a session I had with Paul Lambillion in October 2008.

I asked Martin, through Paul, what he had learned about reincarnation.

As usual Paul seemed to be receiving both words and pictures from Martin. As the following communication came he was concentrating very hard, and constantly checking back to Martin that he was getting the message correctly. He was also commenting on his own understanding of the subject, which is similar to Martin's. For ease of reading I have written the answer as a constant flow of communication, but actually there was a continual struggle to find the right words to express difficult concepts.

"It's a complicated question because he's discovered that what we call *us, ourselves*, is not one thing, it's a composite. The personality is like the glaze on the pot but it's not the pot, and he said that even when we're alive on Earth we're living in more than one dimension at a time even though we're not aware of it. When we're physically here we're still living at other levels of ourselves and in other dimensions. He wants to say that we have a different relationship with time here (on Earth), that the way *we* view time and the way *he* now sees time is slightly different. But he is agreeing that there is soul continuity. That's exactly the words I was given. There's a soul continuity through space and time. That's exactly what I hear and I think he means that the soul has different experiences in different modes and different places. A bit like a spider's web with the soul in the middle, and what we call reincarnation is an aspect of this? (Is that right? Yes, more or less.)

"He says, don't forget that we're viewing this from a three dimensional, intellectual perspective so we're dealing with it in a box. (He's just put it in a box.) But reincarnation is one aspect, one feature of the soul's journey through time and space. And because we have a particular connection with the Earth at the moment, many of us have made these journeys.

"Reincarnation exists but the way it works is slightly more complex than the simplistic way we usually think. The souls journey together in groups through time and space. Clusters of souls. But you don't spend all your life with these souls. You can meet them half way or two thirds of the way through your (Earth) life – someone who's really important to your destiny.

"He showed me all these lights, and they're souls floating together through space and they have a common destiny. And there are a lot of them. Maybe hundreds of souls who have a common destiny. A bit like a cog in a machine. He's affirming that. We do work in this soul-cluster way. Particular roles. Soul clusters. Some kind of on-going connection with the Earth in different forms but not always with a body. He says sometimes the soul will touch the Earth but not physically.

"Another important thing is that when you are closer to your soul, as you are after death, you realise that the soul itself belongs to another kingdom, another dimension, another family. (Paul seems not to understand this and Martin can't explain any more clearly.)

"The souls are likened to stars because souls are like putative stars. He's saying that the soul groups then belong to other groups that link back to the common plane or plateau in which the soul is conscious. But this is what we would call the ineffable, indescribableness of being which we can't get to grips with. I suppose it's like the notion of the over-soul, the collective soul, and all the bits of soul come off it in groups but it's all joined at the super-soul level.

"For us as human beings to think of this is difficult. Our goal is to be alive as souls wherever we are, but the Earth makes it difficult. Whatever words we use are a compromise.

"He said there's cosmic life and planetary life and these two weave together. On the one hand we're working at a high level but part of us is living at this planetary level. These two things work side by side, so that we think this is all there is, whereas the soul knows that it isn't and operates at different levels at the same time.

"Whilst the soul is working through you it's also working beyond you. So it's not confined to you. It has other aspects of its being which are functioning and this ties in with the notion that we can be in more than one place at any given point in space and time but we're not conscious that this is true."

Paul said: "This ties in with what the Ancients believed. The Ancients believed that we are a multiple self. A colony of consciousness and not just one being. We *are* one being but with lots of layers of activity that all interact."

I must admit that all this left me reeling slightly, but I include it because it was obviously important to Martin to get it across. I hope it is helpful. Something to meditate on perhaps.

*

When he was on Earth, Martin said he could remember five past lives, and I would like to tell a little story about an occasion I remember vividly in this connection.

One Saturday night, on the way back to Essex from visiting Martin's parents in Somerset, we stayed in Shaftesbury. On the Sunday morning we set out with the intention of going to Meeting, and found the Meeting House with Friends going in. But suddenly we both decided to walk past. We were used to acting on our hunches so we allowed ourselves to be 'taken' to the ruined Abbey which had a small museum in the entrance area. I walked ahead of Martin and found myself in front of a glass case containing fragments of pottery tiles taken from the floor of the Abbey. As I looked at them I felt a connection with them, and knew that Martin needed to see them. He came to look and was deeply moved. After gazing at them for a while, he went on out into the ruins to recover himself. Very unusually for him, he was in tears.

For years before this he had talked about being a potter in a past life and making tiles for some large ecclesiastical building in the south of England. He had imagined it was a cathedral, because he had thought that at a monastic building the monks would make and lay their own tiles. However, the tiles we had looked at were made in a period when there were nuns at the Abbey. Martin remembered making similar tiles and bringing them in panniers on a packhorse from quite a distance. We later found that there were many small potteries in the nearby area around Salisbury, in the Middle Ages.

*

To venture beyond the early stages of life in the spiritual worlds is not within the scope of this book. The purpose of writing it is to reassure those who doubt and fear death that the next life as described by the communicators is full of sense and purpose and the possibility of progress. Communicators look back at Earth and Earthly beings with a sense of pity. Earth is a training ground in which we learn to deal with the material. It is an essential part of our development, but viewed from a state of higher vibration the dense, heavy nature of the Earth and the relative slowness of movement and communication is obviously quite distasteful to those who have moved on. The 'upwards' that we associate with heaven is actually a raising of vibrational rate rather than of actual height above ground level. Heaven is literally all around us and modern physics can help us to understand how worlds can interpenetrate one another and inhabit the same space. Awakening in the spiritual worlds is often likened to joyfully shedding a deep-sea diving suit!

Those who communicate with us see a little further than we do and their messages can help to uplift us as we journey through life:

Frances Banks again, speaking through Helen Greaves:

I can travel in the mind and this I often do. I have visited countries of the world which I did not know. I have seen much and learned much. I return often to familiar scenes. I attend some Meetings and Meditation Groups and sometimes contact the friends and companions I loved on earth. I do not find it an easy matter to 'speak through' a medium. As you appreciate, I have the conviction that there is no necessity for this. On this level of thought, telepathy is developed to a greater potential than was practised on earth. By means of thought transference, I endeavour to reach the minds of old and dear friends still in physical existence. Sometimes I am happy to think that my efforts meet with a certain response. At others the veil of illusion (even in those who should know better) interferes with reception and the contact is faulty, or is even rejected. But this will be so whilst those on earth still cling to the theory of separativeness.

That which I am learning here, in this wider state of consciousness, is a joyous apprehension of the vast wonder of the unity of Creative Mind in which all, every soul-fragment, every Group Soul, every creative thought, is one.

(Helen Greaves. *Testimony of Light*.)

A prolific writer on Spiritualism during his life, Arthur Findlay communicated after his death, in *More Truth*, stressing the importance he now places on bringing God's love to the world:

I say to you that God's love is an endless chain. One link builds to form strength by joining with another, and so on, till this chain of love is formed. It is a band, a golden band of spiritual understanding. It is not a chain that you would feel was a burden upon you, but a chain that gives you strength and courage to be able to face up to situations, as I, in my own life, have had to face up to situations.

And:

There is so much work here, and so much love for you, my friends. You will never be able to understand the true meaning of God's will and His love. It is only as you progress in spirit to such a level that you are drawn into light that you will truly understand His love and the full meaning of the work that is done here. I have only touched lightly on different subjects because I have felt that it would be unwise to bring too much knowledge, too quickly, because we are all on different levels of thought and it is impossible for all of us to be on the same level at the same time. So there will be many of you, unfortunately who will not be fully able to assimilate and understand the knowledge which will come. But, to the ones who find that they can read my words with an open mind and a thirst for knowledge, then my friends, my endeavour will be to take you further along on the journey with me.

(Eileen Winkworth. *More Truth communicated by Arthur Findlay.)*

In contrast, here is a rather striking quotation from F.W.H. Myers:

It is strange to me that God should be described as loving and good, or as jealous and vengeful. He is none of these. He is the inevitable, the 'Omega' of all life. But He is neither evil nor good, neither cruel nor kind. He is the Purpose behind all purpose. He neither loves nor hates, there is no thought created that expresses Him, for He would seem to me to be all creation and yet apart from it. He is the Idea behind the myriad worlds, behind the unnumbered Universes.

(Geraldine Cummins. *The Road to Immortality communicated by F.W.H. Myers.).*

*

Those we know personally, who communicate with us, are usually in the early stages of spiritual life, often referred to as the planes of form. It is said that the guides who come to offer us help in life, come from the formless realms beyond.

Traditions from both West and East refer to the existence of seven levels or planes above the earth, and although there may be a reassuring glimpse at or near death of one of the more exalted of these levels, it may only actually be reached after further spiritual development at the lower levels. Only those who have already achieved this spiritual development during their earth lives are said to be able to enter it directly.

...Different names are given to these seven planes or levels in the various spiritual traditions and by different communicators, but there seems to be broad agreement that the first four of them are planes of 'form' bearing certain resemblance to life on earth, while the upper three planes are formless realms of increasingly pure and rarefied consciousness.

Communicators inform us that, once in the formless realms, it becomes increasingly difficult to communicate directly with the lower realms of form ...
(David Fontana. *Life Beyond Death: What should we expect?)*

The experience which separates these two sets of planes is described as the second death. Before this occurs, the being undergoes a second life review. David Fontana writes:

This 'second death' is said to involve a boundless elevation of consciousness, as one is now able to move closer to the source of this consciousness. The first death occurred when the soul was separated from the physical body at the end of its earthly existence, and in a second death, the soul separates itself from the illusory body and the illusory world of form. It is said that the second death is much less traumatic than the first, and is undertaken joyfully and only when the individual decides the time is right.

Here is a beautiful quotation from Don Mason's book:

If the reason for our being is to evolve spiritually we are naturally inclined to ask what should be the culmination of this development. All the great religions teach that ultimate perfection is attainable, although a knowledge of in just what form that perfection resides is not accessible to us. Christ's exhortation to 'be perfect even as your Father in heaven is perfect' expresses the Christian belief in this final state of humankind, but if we recognise that God is ineffable and transcendental we cannot conceive of what this state of perfection may be.
(Don Mason, *Science, Mystical Experience and Religious Belief.)*

*

Before finishing this chapter, I must include a little about animal survival. When a cat or dog, or any animal which we have lived closely with, dies, it is like the loss of a family member. The grief can be devastating. When one of my animals dies I always re-read *When Your Animal Dies* by Sylvia Barbanell. And I have lent it to many friends in a similar situation, over the years.

First published in 1940, this little book has been regularly reprinted ever since as it meets a very real need. Not every communication has to be in words, and mediums regularly describe seeing pet animals, dogs, cats, horses coming back to meet and greet their human friends.

Mrs. Florence Kingstone, besides being a great lover of animals, is also a very fine medium. ... She once held a series of séances which were confined only to clairvoyant descriptions of animals.

Because so many people were anxious to know about their pets who had passed on, the medium would only concentrate on the 'dead' animals whom she saw, in order that she might give comfort to their human friends.

On one occasion Mrs. Kingstone saw many spirit forms of animals surrounding one of the sitters. She could not understand the reason for such an assembly of pets, until the woman explained that she was a veterinary surgeon.

She told the medium that her own special pet was among the group of animals that had been described. Mrs. Kingstone not only singled out this favourite dog from the rest, but supplied further evidence by recalling the fact that this animal had met its 'death' through being accidentally shot in the neck by a gamekeeper.

(Sylvia Barbanell. *When Your Animal Dies.*)

It appears that the degree of individuality and self-awareness which an animal attains through contact with humans decides whether or not that animal survives as an individual after death. Herd animals and wild animals, it seems, are assimilated back into a kind of mass Mind. The classic books on psychical research which I have read and which mention animals all make the same kinds of statement. Here is an example from Arthur Findlay as he communicated in *More Truth*.

... never worry over the animals that come into spirit life, for they play, are happy and content, and they join with the ones whom they had joined with on the earth plane (members of families). They are quite content to wait until the one who was their master upon the earth plane passes into spirit so they can be reunited, and until the time comes for them to go back into the big sleep so they can go back into the source of all life to be replenished and re-formed to come in another way.

(Eileen Winkworth. *More Truth communicated by Arthur Findlay.*)

Dogs and cats, particularly cats, are often very psychically aware creatures who seem to see much more in a room than the living occupants. I have given the example of our cat, Prue, and Sylvia Izzard has written about her little dog, Timmy.

Sylvia also gave me an instance of the return of a beloved dog of hers:

Some years ago I visited a medium in London. Towards the end of the session the medium spoke of the presence of a dog in the room, who was wagging his tail. The description he gave completely fitted the Staffordshire bull terrier I had sadly had to have put to sleep a few years before. This part of the session brought a great deal of comfort to me.

Spiritual beings who communicate, regularly describe creatures of all kinds existing in their world. If there were no other sentient beings there I am sure most of us would feel it was not worth going to.

Chapter 14

"Spiritual beings on a human journey"

If you bring forth what is within you, what you bring forth will save you. If you do not bring forth what is within you, what you do not bring forth will destroy you.
Gospel of Thomas

In December 1999, Martin's computer printer was chuntering away through the long dark nights. Being deaf, Martin didn't hear it, but I would lie awake listening, visualising the printed words appearing on the paper.

I was excited, but also extremely apprehensive. Encouraged by Martin, I had written a booklet. It was the culmination of several years of thought, reading and research, and the expression of a real concern to present the *evidence* for life after death as a reality, and something of vital importance that we should understand and discuss while here on Earth.

A local printer produced the simple cover for the booklet, the title *Continuing Life: the evidence for the survival of death through mediumship*, printed on light yellow card – a colour I hoped would appeal to the reader and lift the heart.

The pottery was functioning by this time and in the bedroom above it I used the double bed and a large table to collate and staple the pages of 100 copies of the booklet, while Martin was busy downstairs with the clay.

For far too long I had felt as if I was living in two worlds which had no communicating door. One world contained my Quaker life, which was of the greatest importance to me, the other was one which most Quakers I was in contact with did not seem to know about, or even wish to know about. I found myself unable to tell them of the life I was living in the world of psychic experience, of beautiful, loving communications with spiritual beings which so inspired me. It was becoming an agony to me to have to function in the Quaker world, continually watchful of what I said, censoring my thoughts before they crystallized into words.

Being a natural worrier, I wondered whether launching into print was the right thing to do. And then I read a letter in *The Friend* from someone who was plainly terrified of death and what might come after, and used phrases such as "we cannot know", and "no-one has ever come back to tell us". She was living in one of my worlds but seemed to have no knowledge of the other. It was clear to me once again that I needed to speak out about what I knew.

*

The only group of Quakers I felt I could speak to openly about spiritual/psychic experiences at this time were members of Friends Fellowship of Healing, to which Martin and I had belonged for some years.

David Hodges, a retired biological scientist and university lecturer, and a healer himself, had written books and articles about healing for FFH, and specifically a book about the healing ability of George Fox. I asked him if he would write a foreword for my booklet and he kindly agreed.

His foreword begins as follows:

The fact that Friends seem to have lost contact with their spiritual roots has become a matter of increasing concern within the Society in recent years. Early Friends seemed to live constantly 'In the Light' and their awareness of a greater Spiritual Reality within and beyond themselves enabled them to undertake so much which modern Quakers are often unable to comprehend, let alone carry out. Although much of what they understood and lived out in their lives was expressed in traditional Christian terms, making it even more difficult for many present-day Quakers, the Spiritual Reality which was so real to them needs to be re-explored and recovered by us, their modern counterparts.

To my great delight I discovered that Rosalind Smith was also writing a booklet. The spirit seemed to be moving amongst us! At that time, Ros and her husband, John, were wardens of Claridge House (a Quaker residential centre much used and supported by Friends' Fellowship of Healing members). Ros is the wonderfully supportive F/friend who is editing *this* book for me, and she now takes up the story. It is interesting that she was approaching the subject from a rather different angle. She was discovering that there were many Quakers who were having spiritual/psychic experiences which they did not fully understand and found difficulty in speaking about!

Ros writes:

Some years ago I was involved in offering counselling and healing to Quakers on a fairly regular basis. I soon found that many were seeking help to try and understand why they were having experiences which were, at the time, either unacceptable or hard for them to comprehend. There is very little in Quaker literature which makes any attempt to explain much about life after death, psychic experiences, or spiritual communication from discarnate sources. And yet, the silence which is the integral part of a Meeting for Worship is the ideal place where a person might enter the dimensions which not only surround us, but also interpenetrate our very being.

If we stop to give thought to the masses of radio/TV waves and emanations that exist everywhere, all the time, and are immediately accessible when we have the right equipment to tune in to them, we can perhaps liken them to the even finer frequencies that just await the highly sensitive awareness which is necessary to connect to the spiritual realms. There are people who do have this sensitivity, either as a natural faculty, or because they have been able to recognise it within themselves and then develop it, in the right way. But there have always been those whose motive for developing their psychic 'skills' has not been for the greater good – rather it has been to enhance their own standing with others.

So, as I say, the centring down and entering into the silence which happens at the beginning of a Meeting for Worship is, in effect, similar to the preparation a good medium will undertake when she or he is hoping to communicate with the spirit world. Small wonder, then, that some sensitive Quakers have found that their own awareness has increased, and that they are experiencing the feeling of other presences around them, probably only very slightly but nevertheless noticeable. They may, occasionally, hear with their 'inner ear' something which, if it is meaningful, might be accepted as ministry – all well and good if it is – or, it might just be something personal that they may hold onto, glad that they have been able to receive some help. But, there are times when a definite 'otherness' is observable – either in a clairvoyant or clairaudient way – either during Meeting, or at other times; and many have found this difficult to understand.

I began to be aware that something should be added to

the Friends Fellowship of Healing literature so that those who needed it could have some sort of confirmation that what they were aware of was, in fact, perfectly acceptable, within reason, and that they weren't 'going round the bend' - or needing to put themselves into their nearest psychiatric hospital! So I wrote Quakers and the Spiritual/Psychic Dimension *in 2001, which is now in its third reprint.*

I had decided to write much of it in my garden – it being summer time - and so over a series of sessions I settled down outside. Eventually, I reached the final session which involved finding the right references for the quotes that I had used. This was all fairly straightforward until I tried to find the place in the New Testament that contained the saying 'In Him we live and move and have our being'. I scoured the Gospels, and the Letters etc. but just could not find what I was seeking. It was a very hot day and I decided to give up, and put things aside and have a doze. Just as I was opening a deckchair for myself, a voice flashed into my mind. It said, 'Acts 17'. Now the Acts of the Apostles was one book which I hadn't looked through, feeling that because it was mainly an account of the journeyings of the apostles it would be unlikely to contain what I was looking for. However, I took up the Bible again and went straight to Acts chapter 17. It is a very long chapter and I finally found what I was looking for, near the end, in verse 28. I realised then that I had been receiving help with the writing of this pamphlet! Since it was published I have heard from many Quakers that they have found it very helpful. So I definitely feel that I was 'guided' to write it.

*

I also met Joanna Harris, a great supporter of FFH and Claridge House, and she shared with me her experiences of communication with her husband, Roy, after his sudden, tragic death from a coronary thrombosis at the age of 53, when they were just beginning married life together. Sadly, Joanna died in 2006. Should I say sadly? It is sad for us on Earth, but I think of her now happily reunited with Roy.

What follows is part of Joanna's contribution to the Quaker Anthology we were later to produce:

In 1993 a friend told me about his visit to the College of Psychic Studies in London where a medium put him in touch with his wife, who had died not long before. His wife was happy, and delighted to be in contact. It encouraged me to follow his example and make an appointment, and what I hoped for happened: Roy made contact through the medium, a kind older woman with a lovely voice. From the start I had no doubt that it was Roy communicating through her - what he said about his reactions to what had happened to him was so very much in character.

He told me what a terrible shock his death had been to him. First of all he had to realise that he had died and that was hard, and then that he was alive in a different dimension. If only he had had some warning - he felt it was unfair to have been plucked out of life, and at first he was angry and bitter and he raged against it. But he was given much healing and rest and loving care. My mother spent a lot of time talking with him and that too helped him to come to terms.

He told me that without his body, and the feeling of status he had worked for in life, he felt he was a different being; in fact he felt a speck, a microcosm in the macrocosm. It cost him much effort to accept himself as a spiritual being; only slowly did he get the feeling that the spiritual self is more valuable than the physical self.

He spoke of the colours he was often wrapped around in

– *"The colour is not just a colour, it is a vibration around you and through you, healing and revitalising you. It's wonderful, you know, I have not got over the wonder of it yet."* Roy also told me that our two cats, who had died a few years earlier, were with him, and that my present cat could see him when he was in the house. He wanted me to know that he was always around in the evening when I got ready for bed, and that he wrapped me around with his love as I went to sleep. He felt closer to me now than had been possible in life.

This session with Roy took away any doubts I had about the veracity of this kind of communication. It was so totally true, and it changed my life to know that Roy is around me often, and that we shall meet again in the next life - because love cannot die.

Later, I was given some further assurances of Roy's presence in our house.

One summer evening I had to go out and when I came home it was still light. Walking into the sitting room I was surprised to see a book in the middle of the carpet, closed, standing upright on its long side. As the house had been locked while I was out, there was no way this could have been done by human hand. I felt sure this had to be a signal from Roy - he loved making me laugh, and I did laugh when I saw it was my house plant book. I had not been too successful with some of my plants and was obviously being told I needed to consult the book a bit more!

On a later occasion I saw something very small in a dark corner of the room which certainly had not been there that morning when I hoovered the carpet. It was a pretty cowrie shell with an unusual pattern in violet and brown. Later it was followed, at intervals, by two other small delicate shells which arrived in times of stress, giving me once again the reassurance that I am not alone in the house. Of course I treasure these little *love tokens.*

I have written this because Roy has urged me to. He wanted it known that without any preparation the transition into the next life can be difficult - but that there is help, and all shall be well.

Beryl Spence was another long-standing Quaker friend who was in sympathy with the same ideas, and agreed that they would be taboo in most Quaker Meetings. We had met when we were both committee members of Quaker Concern for Animals. I recently asked her for a contribution to this book and she wrote as follows:

Although I had always had an interest in Spiritualism and a belief in the afterlife, the death of my much loved mother intensified my interest and I hoped for proof of her continued existence. This came to me shortly after she died. A recent present from her had been a generous number of premium bonds and when I protested at the extravagance she had said jokingly, "Well, you can give what you win to me and I'll buy some new curtains." A month later I won a modest amount and while looking sorrowfully at the cheque I suddenly heard her cheerful voice saying, "I'm glad you've had a little win!"

A few months later I had an appointment with a famous psychic artist, Coral Polge, who rapidly produced accurate portraits of my maternal grandmother, grandfather and my little cousin, Joyce, who had died at the age of six. I immediately recognised the other two, but I had not known my grandfather; however, Coral Polge assured me, "He says he's your grandfather," and then, "Why is he putting a gold coin into my hand?" I was wearing a bracelet with a gold coin from my grandfather's watch-chain, but the reference was most probably to his having greeted my newly-born brother with a gold sovereign placed in the baby's hand. Later when I searched through family photographs I found one of my grandfather, looking much younger than in the sketch but recognisably the same person.

My cousin, Joyce, had died of diphtheria at her home in Plymouth within a few weeks of returning from a holiday at our family home in the Isles of Scilly. Coral Polge said of her, "She had a sad little life and I don't mean because she died so young." This was true, as my aunt had always treated her more like a doll than a person, curling her hair, dressing her up and making her sit still and look decorative. After arriving for a visit to Scilly it would be days before she had the confidence to run about on the beach and play games with the rest of us.

There was only one occasion on which I saw what might have been an apparition. This was when I was an adult with a family. I was returning to the house one afternoon and had just put my key into the lock when I saw through a side window a little girl gazing into my vivarium (a heated container used for hatchling tortoises) at the far end of the hall. When I opened the door, she had gone. I thought perhaps it had been my younger daughter but found her with the others in the adjacent room watching children's television. She was surprised to be asked if she had just been looking at the tortoises and said she hadn't.

I had various other convincing experiences, especially when the children were adolescent, but those early ones I found most reassuring and comforting.

The two booklets Ros and I had written gradually began to circulate, and we found that they were producing interest, relief, and a certain sense of excitement that such ideas were being talked about among Quakers. It was very encouraging, and in the summer of 2000, the six of us, Beryl, Joanna, Ros, David, Martin and myself, met at Claridge House to discuss the possibility of setting up a study group.

Ros writes about her feelings at the time:

It was obvious that there was a necessity for a group to be formed which would help to answer the many questions that arise within the Quaker community, and which would prove to be a forum for psychic experiences to be brought into an arena of acceptance and understanding. Such experiences could then be openly discussed, and their value assessed for the individual concerned. Any fear remaining could be dispelled and often a latent ability might be discovered, with the resulting option of whether or not to develop it further.

Of course we had our detractors! This was only to be expected. There are still many people, Quakers and others, who feel that 'dabbling' in the psychic realms is not to be countenanced. They have not taken into account that Jesus himself was psychic, and proved it many times. Also, that throughout the Christian Bible, both New and Old Testaments, there are countless references to spiritual and psychic happenings, which are generally accepted - though the 'witch of Endor' has always had a bad press! (1 Samuel 28: vv.7-25). It has been said by many that if we take the admonition 'turn ye not unto them that have familiar spirits...' (Leviticus 19: v.31) and similar exhortations in Deuteronomy 18: vv.10-12, then we should also take all of the other restrictions placed on people by both of these books. This would include what is said about those we now call gay or lesbian, the children of unmarried mothers, and those who have various sorts of illness and deformity, as well as the restrictions on which meat we should or should not eat. (When I was researching this I found that we are commanded not to eat ostrich! But we now have many ostrich farms around the country. Deuteronomy (again!)14: v.15.) There is a great deal of cruely in the Old Testament, with the ultimate command of 'thine eye shall not pity; life shall go for life, eye for eye, tooth for tooth, hand for hand, foot for foot' (Deuteronomy 19 – v.21).

So, hopefully, we have moved forward from paying too much attention to that ancient regulation which censured any sensitive soul from exercising their skill.

I cannot count the number of people who have said things like "Oh I'm so glad that Quakers have got around to looking into these things!" It seems there is a definite desire among us to learn more about what might happen to us after our physical death. Is there an afterlife? Should we be exploring the possibility that, after all, there just might be more than what meets the eye? Or, should we keep our feet on the ground and attend only to what is happening in the world, channelling our efforts in the direction of helping to create a better and more peaceful environment for the human race? Yes, of course we should be doing that – but, we're all going to die, and there will come a time when each of us has to relinquish our hold on our bodily existence and allow our spiritual essence (or soul) to progress into what we might feel is the 'unknown'. There is a great deal of very helpful literature, written by persons with great integrity after much research and personal experience. We should keep our minds open, while still having our 'feet on the ground', and accept that 'there are more things in heaven and earth, Horatio, than are dreamt of in your philosophy' (Hamlet: Act 1, scene 5).

Personal experience is the key. Once one has glimpsed, even very slightly, the fact of spiritual existence, or received some communication, then there is never any going back to a state of doubt. Any true experience is accompanied by a 'knowing', and from then on one's whole understanding of life is changed. It's really tremendously exciting!

*

It certainly was an exciting time! At that first meeting we

decided on a plan of action for the following year. We would produce an introductory leaflet and a newsletter, and we would invite interested Friends to write about their own spiritual/psychic experiences so that a booklet of these could be published - this was to result in the publication, in 2001, of *The Not Unfamiliar Country: An Anthology of Quaker Experience.*

As we discussed the books we'd read we began to realise how vast the literature on the subject was. We each had our own favourite authors and titles and could hardly believe that in some cases others had not even heard of them.

An idea was born: to write a comprehensive guide. David Hodges set out on this mammoth task which was to occupy him for the next two years and resulted eventually in a unique book of immense value to anyone studying the subject, *Do We Survive Death? A descriptive bibliography and discussion on the evidence supporting survival.*

The name we decided on was Quaker Afterlife Studies Group, later to become Quaker Fellowship for Afterlife Studies as the group grew and stabilised into a more permanent entity. This was not a unanimous, happy choice. There have always been those who would have preferred the title, Quaker Fellowship for Psychical and Spiritual Studies. (They were saying 'my experiences are happening *now* not in the afterlife!*'*) However, the Churches' Fellowship for Psychical and Spiritual Studies already existed and we didn't want to sound as if we were a branch of another organisation.

Over the following months like-minded Friends were attracted to QFAS. Many had been seekers in this area for a large number of years. Jim Shields and George Dobinson were strong supporters with a wide knowledge of psychical research. As an experienced and very gifted medium, Margaret Little gave invaluable advice. There were others who had had significant personal experiences. Elizabeth Angas' near death experience had changed her life, and belonging to QFAS gave her the confidence to write extensively about this in journal and magazine articles. Joan Benner (*Beyond the Music*) and Valerie Cherry (*Light in Death*) had each had very individual experiences of communication with those in the spiritual worlds and have written booklets about them. All these people, without exception, found difficulty in speaking easily in their Quaker Meetings about experiences which were important to them. They had learned when to keep quiet!

In those early days in the life of QFAS, most of us were not really conscious of the fact that we were trying to turn the Society of Friends back towards its roots. We were more concerned with the present and the future, but in fact, in the rich storehouse of Quaker history lay treasure waiting to be re-discovered.

David Hodges had already researched the writings of George Fox and his contemporaries, in order to write his book *George Fox and the Healing Ministry*.

QFAS now attracted to its membership historian David Britton, who came up with some gems from the same period. The words which follow he found in Fox's *Book of Miracles:*

George Fox's mother died in 1674, when Fox was in Worcester gaol, and was prevented from visiting her. When the letter about her death reached him, he was grieved, but – "When my spirit had gotten through I saw her in the resurrection and the life, everlastingly with me, and father in the flesh also."
(Henry J. Cadbury, *George Fox's Book of Miracles)*

David also discovered Pendle Hill pamphlet 340, *The Quaker Way of Dying,* by Lucy Screechfield McIver, which was full of beautiful and highly pertinent quotations, some of which follow:

This night or tomorrow night I shall depart hence...Do not seek to hold me for it is too strait for me; and out of this straitness[3] I must go, for I am wound into largeness.

These are the words of the seventeenth century Quaker, Richard Hubberthorne, when he was approaching his death. With what confidence Hubberthorne approached the end of his physical life, and what a wonderful feeling of enlargement and expansion he was expecting to enter into! This reflects the hope and confidence which was generally apparent in the early Quakers. They took the spiritual worlds for granted and so full of hardship were their lives on Earth, frequently involving persecution, imprisonment, long arduous journeys travelling in the ministry, and illness, that often death came almost as a welcome release.

Margaret Fell outlived her second husband, George Fox, by eleven years. Here is what she wrote in his Testimony, when he died in 1691:

It has pleased God to take away my dear husband out of this evil troublesome world, who was not a man thereof, being chosen out of it, and had his life and being in another region...so I am now to give my account and testimony for my dear husband, whom the Lord has taken unto his blessed kingdom and glory... Now he has finished his course and his testimony, and is entered into his eternal rest and felicity. (Ibid)

William Penn's twenty-one year old son, Springette, had wished to travel in the ministry with his father, but he was ill and nearing death. Penn comforted his son with these beautiful words:

My dear child, if it please the Lord to raise thee, I am satisfied it will be so; and if not, then in as much as it is thy

---

[3] 'Strait' meaning 'narrow'.

fervent desire in the Lord, he will look upon thee just as if thou didst live to serve him, and thy comfort will be the same. So, either way, it will be well; for if thou shouldst not live, I do verily believe thou wilt have the recompense of thy good desires, without the temptations and troubles that would attend if long life were granted to thee.

At this, we are told;

... Springette surrendered his desire and replied to his father: "My eye looks another way, where the truest pleasure is... All is mercy, dear father, everything is mercy." (Ibid)

What a vision the young man must have beheld when he allowed himself to contemplate his death.

The early Quakers had little fear of death and prepared themselves thoroughly, ministering to those around them as if in a special position of authority.

A devout Quaker lived every day as if it were the last. Death was the climax to life: the period just before the end was supposed to reveal either the righteous prevailing and triumphant, or the wicked filled with fear and repenting. The dying person, neither fully part of this world nor yet joined to the next, could speak to those around with an authority possessed by no ordinary person. An entire household gathered in the death chamber to hear the final words of exhortation. Many visitors, including young children, would gather around the dying individual who, in their closest relationship to God, would preach to them.

The contemporary perspective differs from that of seventeenth-century Quakers. We do not know how to speak of death, to ourselves, to each other, or to our children. Often we find our loved ones painfully alone in hospital rooms with family and friends, either resisting death's imminence, or not knowing how to offer comfort and support. (Ibid)

*

In 2007 Jan Arriens, writer and former diplomat who was by now on the QFAS committee, gave a talk at the Spring Conference. In this extract from his opening remarks he is referring to the early Quakers:

I have been struck by the extent to which psychic phenomena and what we now term extrasensory perception were interwoven into their lives and faith. Like people in the Bible, they heard voices and had visions that changed their lives. They took dreams seriously and acted upon them. Quakerism would not have come about without the 'great openings' described by George Fox. Acting on leadings, Robert Fowler crossed the Atlantic with 11 friends on board in his coastal vessel the Woodhouse; John Woolman felt impelled to visit chief Papunahung at a dangerous time; Stephen Grellet had a vision on Long Island that changed his life, ultimately affecting Elizabeth Fry and prison reform. Later Quakers too, such as Rufus Jones upon the death of his son, and Caroline Stephen had profound mystical openings.

Jan went on to analyse what he feels has happened to the Religious Society of Friends in the intervening three hundred years or so.

There are two main reasons why attitudes differ from those of earlier times. We live in a rational, post-Darwinian scientific age. We have looked back at the Earth from far out into space. Modern scientific knowledge can encourage us to look away from ideas of God and any higher form of collective consciousness. Such thinking is behind much of the scepticism or indifference towards psychic phenomena that we find in the Society of Friends today.

The second reason is that, very much to their credit, Friends have never set much store by the afterlife. Even in the early days of Quakerism, the concern was much more with the here and now than with storing up any reward in heaven. Quakers have never been particularly concerned about the resurrection or the doctrines of redemption and atonement. Instead, the emphasis has been on direct revelation, individual discernment, collective discernment, and collective worship.

Perhaps rather than worrying too much about the reason why Quaker belief may have suffered the changes it has, QFAS should look to the future and simply continue to state quietly but insistently that spiritual/psychic experiences occur in the lives of Friends as they do in the lives of all human beings, and that, while they may not always seem significant when looked at in isolation, taken together they have immense importance and give us strong intimations of our immortality.

If the prevalence of a dogmatic 'scientific' view has been part of the problem, things are gradually changing. In recent years two Quaker scientists have published books accepting the existence of life beyond death. Don Mason (Emeritus Professor of Immunology, Oxford University), wrote *Science, Mystical Experience and Religious Belief* in 2006, from which I have quoted earlier, and Bob Anderson, a New Zealand Friend (with a PhD in science education and a combined honours degree in physics and chemistry) wrote *You Can't Die for the Life of You!* in 2008.

*

Ten years have passed and QFAS is now a Listed Informal Group of Britain Yearly Meeting. Ten day conferences have been held in London, and ten residential conferences, all, until 2009, at Claridge House. We've explored many aspects of spiritual/psychic experience, and heard fascinating speakers, but the most popular part of the programme always seems to be the time spent in personal or group sharing. Everyone comes bursting to talk and ask questions in an accepting atmosphere, and animated conversation breaks out in any available free time. It truly does feel like a fellowship.

In July 2009 we hosted a larger than usual conference at Woodbrooke Quaker Study Centre. I arrived in Birmingham a day early so that I could talk to the staff and make some preparations. At supper I sat next to a woman Friend in her eighties, who was recovering from the death of her husband and her own illness; there were just the two of us at the table. She asked me which conference I was attending and, when I explained she looked shocked, and said that I only believed in "that sort of thing" because I *wanted* to. She made disparaging remarks about mediums and then said firmly, about her husband, "He's dead, gone. It's finished".

We agreed to change the subject and spoke about other things until the meal was over, when I left the table as quickly as I could, feeling within myself a deep inner chill. It was a salutary lesson to me. QFAS certainly has a job to do!

The conference was a success.

*

In September 09, I visited Paul Lambillion taking for him a typescript of this book, as far as I had written it then. This included everything I had typed back from our sessions together which I proposed to use. I asked him to read it through during the next few weeks and let me know if he was happy with what I had written. After some conversation, Paul said that Martin was around wearing his Flower Pot Man's hat, and he asked Martin if he wanted to communicate on any important issues or ideas.

Of course he did!

As usual, there was quite a long pause as Paul listened. Then he said that Martin approved of the book:

"He says, 'Very good. Get it reviewed. And not just in the Quaker press.'"

Then Paul added, in surprise: "Oh, chapter seven. He's being quite specific here. Chapter seven. They showed me a map."

I was amazed that Martin should refer to the text in such detail!

"What's chapter seven about?" said Paul, leafing rapidly through the sheets, "I didn't quite expect this."

"Neither did I," I said. "Does he want to change something?"

Paul found the chapter and asked Martin what he wanted to say. There was another long pause and then Paul said, "Esperantist. Did you know Edward Osmotherley?"

"Yes, I did."

"Martin's met his soul since he went over." Paul searched through the typescript and found the reference from the session in 2004, just after I had burnt Edward's Esperanto writings. (See page 73)

There was a bit more confusion about what the communication meant, and a bit more listening, and then Paul suddenly seemed to grasp it.

"I think Edward was a clever man. He's been especially interested in your writing and has been trying to be creative. He says in a funny kind of way you're trying to give people another language for understanding…another text…another way of looking at life."

I thought this was a lovely message, especially from someone whose work I had destroyed! But then Edward was/is an exceptionally wise and loving man. I am delighted to know that he is helping me.

*

In October of 2009, QFAS committee member, Roger Straughan (formerly Reader in Education at Reading University, and an established author in his own field) published a book about his experience of communication with Arthur Conan Doyle, called *A Study in Survival: Conan Doyle Solves the Final Problem.*

In November of 2009, suddenly realizing that 2010 would mark the tenth year of the existence of QFAS, the committee decided to write a statement. Emails flew to and fro and eventually we came up with a wording we could all agree on. We decided to come out strongly and state our acceptance of life after death as fact. What follows is the conclusion to what we wrote:

The QFAS Conference at Woodbrooke, 2009, was entitled, 'The Afterlife: How good is the evidence?' The answer, we decided, is: 'very good indeed. And very empowering.'

One cannot continue to look at evidence for ever. Sooner or later a verdict has to be reached. So the committee agree that the time has come to move on, and in the next ten years of the life of QFAS to take our 'verdict' to a wider audience with confidence and fresh energy.

The reason for this, of course, is to help people overcome the debilitating fear of death! Knowledge about life beyond death can bring comfort and reassurance to those approaching their own death or that of family members; and for younger people it can bring a new sense of meaning and purpose, once physical life is seen as part of a greater whole. We believe that the existence of life beyond death is a truth, and that an understanding of this truth is part of our birthright, and not something which should remain hidden.

Belief in an afterlife is linked to no particular religion. We believe that a large body of overwhelming evidence has accumulated over many years clearly indicating the survival of the human personality. One day we hope that the strength of this evidence will be widely accepted.

But don't take our word for any of this! The only way forward is to set out on your own voyage of discovery and see where it leads you.

*

It is now January, 2010. My story has reached the present time, and this book is reaching its conclusion. Why was writing it so important to me?

In 2009, the bicentenary of Charles Darwin's birth was celebrated. There were new books, there were articles, TV and radio programmes galore, telling of his achievements. What was Darwin's work concerned with? Discovering and explaining to humanity where we have come from, in a *physical* sense. It was concerned with the *vehicle* which houses the soul while on Earth.

In the same century that Darwin and others were writing about the physical origin of species, communications from the spiritual worlds were beginning to reach humanity. They gave us information about our *other vital component, the soul.* Body and soul, which is more important? We inhabit the body for a short space of time, the soul is immortal, our link to the spiritual dimensions. But when, in our materialistic world, do we read serious articles, or see sensible (not sensational and distorted) TV programmes on the subject of the spiritual/psychic communications? I wait in hope!

*

It is important for our loved ones to be able to reassure us that they are in a new life in which we shall one day join them. Important for them and for us. We will still grieve for them, of course, but knowing that they live on and that the links of love are not broken or changed in any way is a tremendous comfort and support, as I, and many others, know from personal experience.

It is important that we are aware of our guides, the more advanced souls who will help us with teaching and with love. The spiritual beings living in their realm are able to inspire us with the ideas humanity so desperately needs. They are ready and willing if we will only listen.

It is important for young people to know who they really are, to be able to link safely from an early age to a spiritual world they can understand and trust to support them through their Earthly journey. It is their birthright. I have seen a beautiful response in a young person to a communication through a medium from a much loved grandfather. The grandfather was concerned that this boy, in his late teens, was getting into bad company, and asked him to think more carefully when choosing his friends. After the initial embarrassment and confusion at hearing from his grandfather in another dimension, the boy's face lit up. He nodded, ruefully. He understood. Someone cared about him. The young need to be aware that they are surrounded by loving carers as they face up to the challenges of life.

It is important that the old, who are approaching death, have the knowledge to face their future with confidence and be ready to greet their loved ones who will come to help them across when the time comes for them to enter their new life.

I am very fortunate. I have had wonderful evidence for the survival of human and animal personality beyond death. I felt that this was worth writing about as it might help others. Naturally I hope that this book has some value of itself, but more than that I hope that it may link you with the wealth of literature on this subject and with the wide world of spiritual experience from which it has come to us.

In order to live to the fullest we need to see our life on Earth for what it really is, an episode in the development of a soul.

Booklist

Barbanell, Sylvia,
- *When Your Animal Dies,* First pub. Spiritualist Press, 1942. Reprinted Spiritual Truth Foundation, 2002. ISBN 0-85437-014-5
- *When a Child Dies.* First pub. Psychic Press, 1942. Reprinted Pilgrim Books, 1984. ISBN 0-946259-08-9

Bassett, Jean, *100 Years of National Spiritualism.* The Headquarters Publishing Co. Ltd.,1990. ISBN 0-947823-20-4

Beard, Paul,
- *Survival of Death.* 1966. Reprinted Pilgrim Books, 1988.
ISBN 0-946259-25-9
- *Living On.* 1980. Reprinted Pilgrim Books, 1987. ISBN 0-946259-24-0
- *Hidden Man.* Pilgrim Books, 1986. ISBN 0-946259-16-X

Butler, W.E., *How to Read the Aura.* The Aquarian Press, 1971

Cadbury, Henry J., *George Fox's Book of Miracles.* Cambridge University Press, 1948.

Conan Doyle, Arthur, *History of Spiritualism (2 volumes).* First pub. 1926. Reprinted by The Spiritual Truth Press, 2008. ISBN 978-0-85384-110-4

Cummins, Geraldine,
- *The Road to Immortality. Being a description of the After-life purporting to be communicated by the late F.W.H Myers.* Ivor Nicholson & Watson, Ltd., 1933.
- *Swan on a Black Sea.* Routledge & Kegan Paul, 1965.

Fenwick, Peter & Elizabeth, *The Art of Dying.* Continuum, 2008.
ISBN 978-08264-9923-3

Findlay, Arthur, *The Rock of Truth,* Psychic Press, 1933.
- See also Winkworth, Eileen. *More Truth communicated by Arthur Findlay.*

Fontana, David,
- *Is There an Afterlife? A Comprehensive Overview of the Evidence,* O-Books, 2005 (for theory of Super-ESP see pages 103-113). ISBN 1-903816-90-4
- *Life Beyond Death: What Should We Expect?* Watkins, 2009.
ISBN 978-1-905857-97-5

Galloway, Donald, *Inevitable Journey,* Con-Psy Publications, 1994.

Greaves, Helen, *Testimony of Light,* World Fellowship Press for the Churches' Fellowship for Psychical and Spiritual Studies, 1969.
ISBN 0-85435-1647-239

Hodges, David,
- *George Fox and the Healing Ministry.* Pub. Friends' Fellowship of Healing, 1995.
- *Do We Survive Death? A descriptive bibliography on the evidence supporting survival,* 2004. ISBN. 0-9546122-0-5.
Available from David Hodges, 14 Eythorne Close, Kennington, Ashford, Kent, TN24 9LP.

Humann, Harvey, *Death Without Fear.* Penthe Publishing Co. Kansas, 1992. ISBN 0-9632475-6-5

Inskip, Jill,
Harris, Joanna, contributions to, *The Not Unfamiliar Country: Communication Beyond Death, An Anthology of Quaker Experience,* Webb's Cottage Press, 2001. ISBN 978-1-899391-10-3.
Available from Quaker Fellowship for Afterlife Studies, Webb's Cottage, Woolpits Road, Saling, Braintree, Essex, CM7 5DZ.

Lambillion, Paul
- *How to Heal and Be Healed.* Gateway/Gill and Macmillan, currently out of print.
- *Auras and Colours – A Guide to Subtle Energies*, Gateway/Gill & MacMillan. ISBN 0-7171-3232-3
- *Staying Cool, A De-Stressing Guide for Young People.* Newleaf/Gill & MacMillan.
- *Communications from Heartstar through Paul Lambillion.* Paul Lambillion. L.N. Fowler & Co Ltd, 1993. ISBN 0-85243-795-1.
Paul Lambillion, 120 Appledown Drive, Bury St. Edmunds, Suffolk, IP32 7HQ. Phone 01284-764780. www.paullambillion.co.uk
Also available - CDs and flower essences.

Lehmann, Rosamund, *The Swan in the Evening. Fragments of an inner life.* First pub. Collins, 1967. Reprinted Virago Press, 1982. ISBN 0-86068-299.
*The Awakening Letters (*Co-author Cynthia Sandys). First pub. Neville Spearman, 1978. Reprinted by C.W. Daniel, 1986

Lodge, Oliver, *Raymond Revised* A new and abbreviated edition of *Raymond or Life After Death* with an additional chapter, Methuen & Co., 1922.

Mason, Don, *Science Mystical Experience and Religious Truth,* Sessions, 2006. ISBN 1-85072-357-5.
Available from Don Mason, 5 Larch Lane, Witney, Oxon, OX28 1AG.

McIver, Lucy Screechfield, Pendle Hill pamphlet 340, *The Quaker Way of Dying.*

Northage, Ivy, *Mediumship Made Simple,* Psychic Press, 1986.

Rodegast, Pat and Stanton, Judith (compilers),
- *Emmanuel's Book: A manual for living comfortably in the cosmos.* 1987. ISBN 0-553-34387-4
- *Emmanuel's Book II: The choice for love.* 1989. ISBN 0-553-34750-0.
Bantam Books.

Rose, Aubrey, *Journey into Immortality.* Lennard Publishing, 1997. ISBN 1-85291-133-6

Sherwood, Jane,
- *Peter's Gate: a Book for the Elderly* First pub. CFPSS, 1973. Reprinted C.W.Daniel, 1992. ISBN 0-85207-259-7
- *The Four-Fold Vision.* Neville Spearman Ltd., 1965
- *The Country Beyond.* First pub. Neville Spearman Ltd, 1969. Reprinted C.W.Daniel, 1991. ISBN 0-85207-254-6
- *Post-Mortem Journal.* Communications from T.E. Lawrence. Neville Spearman Ltd., 1964. Reprinted 1976.
- Edition combining *The Psychic Bridge* and *The Country Beyond*, 1969.

Shine, Betty, *Mind to Mind,* Bantam Books, 1989. ISBN 0-593-01525-6
Mind Magic. Corgi books London. ISBN 0-552-13671-9

White, Ruth,
- *Gildas Communicates*
- *Seven Inner Journeys*
- *The Healing Spectrum*
- *A Question of Guidance.* C.W. Daniel, 1988. ISBN 0-85207-193-0

Winkworth, Eileen. *More Truth communicated by Arthur Findlay.* Harmony Press Ltd, 1985. ISBN 0-946899-01-0.

Suggested further reading and other information

Anderson, Bob, *You Can't Die for the Life of You!* Bob Anderson. R.G. and J. Anderson, 2008. ISBN 978-0-473-13157-9. (Not at present available in the UK.)

Benner, Joan, *Beyond the Music.* Available from Joan Benner, 12 Manor Gardens, Hampton, Middx., TW12 2TU.

Bloom, William, *The Endorphin Effect: A breakthrough strategy for holistic and spiritual wellbeing.* Piatkus, 2001. ISBN 0749-921-1587.

Cherry, Valerie, *Light in Death.* Available from Valerie Cherry, Garden House, Bonfire Lane, Woodbury, Exeter, EX5 1HT.

Ellison, Arthur, *The Reality of the Paranormal.* The Guild of Publishing by arrangement with Harrap Ltd., 1988. ISBN 0-245-54474-7

The Findhorn Foundation. There are many books published by Findhorn Publications, The Park, Forres, 1V36 0TZ, Scotland. Among them are two booklets The Living Word and Footprints on the Path by Eileen Caddy. www.Findhorn.org

Foy, Robin P., *In Pursuit of Physical Mediumship.* Janus Publishing Co., 1996. ISBN 1-85756-248-8

Graff, Dale E., *Tracks in the Psychic Wilderness: An exploration of remote viewing, ESP, pre-cognition, dreaming and synchronicity.* Element, 1998. ISBN 186-204-3515.

Hancock, Sheila, *The Two of Us: My Life with John Thaw.* Bloomsbury, 2004. ISBN 0-7475-7020-5

Hunniford, Gloria, *Next to You: Caron's Courage Remembered by her Mother.* Michael Joseph, 2005. ISBN 0-718-14842-8

Kübler-Ross, Elisabeth, *Death is of Vital Importance: On Life, Death and Life After Death,* Station Hill Press, 1995. ISBN 0-88268-186-9. And many other titles.

Myers, F.W.H., *Human Personality and its Survival of Bodily Death.* First pub. Longmans Green, 1903. An abridged version appeared in 1919. Abridged version reprinted by Pilgrim Books,1992. ISBN 0-946-259-39-39

McTaggart, Lynne, *The Field: The quest for the secret force of the universe.* Element, 2003. ISBN 0007-145-101.

Morse, Melvin, *Closer to the Light: Learning from Children's Near-Death Experiences.* First pub. in the USA by Villard Books, New York, 1990. First British edition, Souvenir Press Ltd., 1991. ISBN 0-285-63030 X

Neate, Tony
- *The Guide Book.* Channelled by Tony Neate. Gateway Books, 19 Circus Path, Bath, BA1 2PW, 1986. ISBN 0-946551-33-2
- *H.A. on Life and Living.* Channelled by Tony Neate and Diane Furlong. Pegasus Foundation, 1992. ISBN 0-9519827-1-0

Polge, Coral, *The Living Image,* Regency Press, 1985. Re-printed as *Living Images*, 1991, 1997. ISBN 0-900697-17-2

Smith, Rosalind, *Quakers and the Spiritual/Psychic Dimension*. Available from Friends Fellowship of Healing: Alan Pearce, 15 East Street, Bluntisham, Huntingdon, Cambs, PE28 3LS.

Straughan, Roger, *A Study in Survival: Conan Doyle Solves the Final Problem*. O-Books, 2009. ISBN 978-1-84694-240-2.

Walsch, Neale Donald, *The New Revelations: A Conversation with God*. Hodder and Stoughton, 2003. ISBN 0-340-82590-1.

White Eagle Lodge, New Lands, Liss, Hampshire, GU33 7HY. There are many books published by The White Eagle Publishing Trust. 15 booklets of White Eagle's teachings. www.whiteagle.org. Journal, *Stella Polaris*.

Organisations.

The Alister Hardy Society, Religious Experience Research Centre, Dept of Theology and Religious Studies, University of Wales, Lampeter, Ceredigion, SA48 7ED. www.alisterhardyreligiousexperiences.co.uk
Email:ahardytrust@lamp.ac.uk

The Arthur Findlay College, Stansted Hall, Stansted, Essex, CM24 8UD. www.snu.org.uk Phone: 01279-813636

Bristol Cancer Help Centre, Grove House, Cornwallis Gove, Bristol, BS8 4PG. Helpline: helpline@bristolcancerhelp.org. Phone: 0845-123-23-10

The Churches Fellowship for Psychical and Spiritual Studies, The Rural Workshop, South Road, North Somercotes, Lincs, LN11 7PT. www.churchesfellowship.org.uk Phone: 01507-358845

CRUSE. www.Crusebeareavementcare.org.uk.

The Leslie Flint Educational Trust, 13 Pembridge Place, London, W2 4XB. www.leslieflint.com Email. info@leslieflint.com.

Society for Psychical Research, 49 Marloes Rd, London, W8 6LA. www.spr.ac.uk

The College of Psychic Studies, 16 Queensberry Place, London, SW7 2EB. www.collegeofpsychicstudies.co.uk. Phone: 020-7589-3292/3

Quaker Fellowship for Afterlife Studies, clerk, Angela Howard, Webb's Cottage, Woolpits Road, Saling, Braintree, Essex, CM7 5DZ. www. quakerfellowshipforafterlifestudies

The Spiritualist Association of Great Britain, 33 Belgrave Square, London, SW1X 8QB. www.sagb.org.uk Phone: 020-7235-3351

Quaker Terminology

Ministry.
Various forms of service to which the gifts (spiritual and other) of the individual may be matched.

Vocal ministry. (Pages 12 & 15)
It is part of the Quaker tradition from the beginning, that during a meeting for worship anyone may rise to speak or to pray....Vocal ministry has been described as "the offering of experience won in thought and in life which ...has led to a deeper vision of God."

Testimonies to the Grace of God in the life of a Quaker. (Pages 82 & 231)
Since the earliest days of Quakerism, accounts of the life and spiritual journey of a Friend have been written after their death and read aloud in Meetings.

Our custom of writing testimonies to the grace of God as shown in the lives of Friends provides us with a wealth of material showing ordinary Friends living out their faith from day to day. These testimonies show us that, whatever our circumstances, God can be present with us, and they encourage us each to be faithful to our own calling.
Quaker Faith and Practice, introduction to Chapter 18.

Thaxted Monthly Meeting (Page 82)
A monthly meeting for Friends of several Local Quaker Meetings in North Essex for worship and to conduct business. These meetings are held less frequently nowadays and are known as Area Meetings.

Essex and Suffolk General Meeting (Page 103)
A gathering of Friends from the two counties which meets usually three times a year to worship together and listen to a talk. Now known as a Regional Gathering.

These meetings are part of the structural organisation for Friends' meetings established in the seventeenth century for the area covered by **Britain Yearly Meeting.**

(Quaker Speak *by Alistair Heron, 1994, revised and republished in a fourth edition by Quaker Outreach in Yorkshire, in 2008, has been very helpful to me in attempting these definitions.)*